THE GOFAST GUIDE TO SCREENWRITING

Creator of the GoFaSt Model, author Greg Takoudes introduces a comprehensive study of the structural models of screenwriting and provides readers with an adaptive framework for writing successful scripts.

With a new approach that reframes discussions and offers alternatives to students and writers who find conventional models creatively constricting, Takoudes draws from both teaching and professional experience to provide a new model of screenwriting that is designed to be adaptive to various types of scripts. The book is structured in three parts. First, it introduces the GoFaSt Model – allowing for less orthodox writers to keep their unique voices by breaking scripts down into smaller parts and encouraging more flexibility to write in an organized way, without feeling stifled. Second, the book explores several writing scenarios – featuring the practical uses of the model and a step-by-step script structure spanning chapters on a horror, superhero, and heist movie. Third, it concludes with detailed case studies exploring how the GoFaSt Model can be applied to break down scripts including *Get Out*, *The Marvelous Mrs. Maisel*, and *Portrait of a Lady on Fire*.

It is an ideal text for screenwriting students and aspiring screenwriters interested in learning how working writers put structural models into practice, as well as professional screenwriters, producers, and development executives looking for new ways to think about writing, feedback, and development.

Greg Takoudes is a filmmaker and screenwriter and Adjunct Professor of Film Studies at The New School, New York. His feature film *Up With Me*, distributed by IFC Films, premiered at South by Southwest, where it won the Special Jury Award, was played at film festivals in America and Europe. His debut novel *When We Wuz Famous* was published by Henry Holt/Macmillan, and he previously worked for Ron Howard and Brian Grazer as a member of the creative team at Imagine Entertainment. For more information, visit www.takoudes.com.

THE GOFAST GUIDE TO SCREENWRITING

The Goals, Failures and Stakes Model of Narrative Storytelling

Greg Takoudes

LONDON AND NEW YORK

Designed cover image: © Getty Images

First published 2024
by Routledge
4 Park Square, Milton Park, Abingdon, Oxon OX14 4RN

and by Routledge
605 Third Avenue, New York, NY 10158

Routledge is an imprint of the Taylor & Francis Group, an informa business

© 2024 Greg Takoudes

The right of Greg Takoudes to be identified as author of this work has been asserted in accordance with sections 77 and 78 of the Copyright, Designs and Patents Act 1988.

All rights reserved. No part of this book may be reprinted or reproduced or utilised in any form or by any electronic, mechanical, or other means, now known or hereafter invented, including photocopying and recording, or in any information storage or retrieval system, without permission in writing from the publishers.

Trademark notice: Product or corporate names may be trademarks or registered trademarks, and are used only for identification and explanation without intent to infringe.

British Library Cataloguing-in-Publication Data
A catalogue record for this book is available from the British Library

Library of Congress Cataloging-in-Publication Data
Names: Takoudes, Greg, author.
Title: The GoFaSt guide to screenwriting : the goals, failures
   and stakes model of narrative storytelling / Greg Takoudes.
Description: Abingdon, Oxon ; New York, NY : Routledge, 2024. |
   Includes bibliographical references and index.
Identifiers: LCCN 2023024784 (print) | LCCN 2023024785 (ebook) |
   ISBN 9780367693701 (hardback) | ISBN 9780367693695 (paperback) |
   ISBN 9781003141549 (ebook)
Subjects: LCSH: Motion picture authorship.
Classification: LCC PN1996 .T255 2024 (print) | LCC PN1996
   (ebook) | DDC 808.2/3—dc23/eng/20230706
LC record available at https://lccn.loc.gov/2023024784
LC ebook record available at https://lccn.loc.gov/2023024785

ISBN: 978-0-367-69370-1 (hbk)
ISBN: 978-0-367-69369-5 (pbk)
ISBN: 978-1-003-14154-9 (ebk)

DOI: 10.4324/9781003141549

Typeset in Sabon
by Apex CoVantage, LLC

CONTENTS

1 An Introduction   1

2 Goals   11

3 Failures   24

4 Stakes   35

5 GoFaSt Exercise: Writing a Sample Horror Movie   46

6 GoFaSt Exercise: Writing a Sample Superhero Movie   57

7 GoFaSt Exercise: Writing a Sample Heist Movie   69

8 GoFaSt Case Study: There Will Be Blood   78

9 GoFaSt Case Study: Get Out   91

10 GoFaSt Case Study: Portrait of a Lady on Fire   100

11 GoFaSt Case Study: The Marvelous Mrs. Maisel   109

12 Conclusion   119

Index   *122*

The GoFaSt Guide to Screenwriting

1

AN INTRODUCTION

As both a filmmaker and an educator of filmmaking, I am fascinated by the countless decisions that go into making a movie. From casting to locations to camera angles to props to costumes to every other decision, both creative and logistical, how does the filmmaker know the correct choices to make?

One basis for decision-making is the aesthetic tastes and instincts of the filmmaker. They will judge, by watching rehearsals or the footage on the monitor, whether the shots look right and what adjustments need to be made. Sometimes the reasons for those adjustments can be articulated, and other times they cannot, because it is creative instinct driving the choices. Another basis for decision-making is the production and budgetary limitations of the film: the number of days allowed to film a certain location, the hours of sunlight remaining in the day, and the equipment available on production all guide the decisions that a filmmaker makes. However, perhaps the most significant basis for making these decisions – and the concern of this book – is the demands of the screenplay.

The screenplay is the bedrock of filmmaking. It has often been said that the ceiling for how "good" a film can be is usually set by, and limited to, the quality of the script. Regardless of the brilliance of the direction, and deftness of the performances, a mediocre script will usually produce, at best, a mediocre film. The problems that exist in the script – whether the issues are structural, or problems in character development, or poorly written dialogue – will continue to be problems in production and remain permanently as problems in the film after post-production is complete. It is very hard – and usually requires time, expense, and luck – to fix problems in the screenplay during any other phase of filmmaking than the screenwriting itself.

2 An Introduction

For the screenwriter, the weight of this responsibility might sound scary. But it is not.

Perhaps it is better to take this warning as inspiration. A well-written script gives actors the ability to do their best work and frees the director to be fully creative by knowing that the bones of the narrative are solid and trustworthy, and the director will not need to spend time and energy avoiding potholes embedded in the script pages. The better the script, the more comfortable and inspired everyone on set feels. Indeed, the entire process of filmmaking rests on those slim one hundred or so pages, modestly set together with a pair of brads.

In my work as a filmmaker and university lecturer, the nature of screenwriting – and the mysterious and much-analyzed process by which scripts are written and can be improved – has preoccupied me.

The inspiration for this book, *The GoFaSt Guide to Screenwriting*, originated years ago during one of my first jobs in the film industry. I worked at a development company in Los Angeles. Script development companies are concerned with seeking out and acquiring scripts, and then improving the scripts through many rounds of rewrites, by giving notes and suggestions to the writers, and finally attaching key creative personnel to the movie and sending it off to production. Once the writer is finished writing, development is where the movie-making machinery begins.

As the normal practice goes, most scripts that are submitted to a development company will receive a coverage report. Coverage reports are the currency of the development world, assigning value to scripts by rating and grading them. Prepared by a reader who is hired by the company, coverages usually contain two pages of plot summary, and one page of analysis describing the strengths and weaknesses of a script.

At the company where I worked, the sheer amount of coverage reports we accumulated was staggering. This being the pre-digital era, our coverages were kept in cabinets. Each cabinet drawer held thousands of coverages, and every cabinet held three drawers. Given that there were over a dozen of these enormous cabinets in the backrooms of our offices, which gives a sense of just how many scripts were submitted over the years.

During off-hours, I would skim these coverages. I had reverence for each coverage because every script represented months or years of a writer's time, and ambitions for being a working writer, and here they were – untold thousands – archived in summary form in a drawer that resembled catacombs. The first page of a coverage includes the logline of the script: a one- or two-sentence description of the storyline. In the time that I spent browsing through the coverages, I had two takeaways.

First, I could not help but notice just how much promise there was in the majority of scripts. Great concepts abounded in the logline descriptions, and many of the analyses discussed characters or sequences in the scripts that seemed creative, exciting, heartfelt, and generally worked quite well.

Second, almost every coverage report concluded with a recommendation to "pass" – that is, reject – the script. This is not surprising: most scripts do not get produced. The sheer volume of rejections creates an impression that most scripts are not worthwhile. But I disagree with this assumption. The uncommon truth of screenwriting is that there is an enormous amount of excellent movie ideas out there. The cynics of the film industry would believe that most screenwriters are "hacks," and most scripts are hopelessly bad. However, during my time working in development, and during my years teaching screenwriting, script analysis, and film production at The New School, a university in New York City, I have developed an irrevocable optimism about many of the scripts and screenwriters that have come my way.

There is an inspiring amount of good – and potentially great – material out there. The overriding limitation that many screenwriters experience has less to do with the quality of the stories these writers want to tell, or their ability to tell them – rather, it is the lack of tools for *how* to tell their stories.

Of course, university screenwriting classes and books on screenwriting offer no shortage of tools. Three-act structure, four-act structure, the hero's journey, etc. – these staples, among others, of the screenwriting structural universe – help writers uncover the *how*, but to a limited degree. All of these tools have limitations themselves and inherent traps that can steer the screenwriter into overly formulaic territory and create scripts that lack organic flair and dampen each writer's unique voice.

Moreover, the tools – though based on the timeless traditions of storytelling that originate from mythic fables to Aristotle to today's greatest scripts – can fall short of connecting with the voices of new, young writers looking to tell stories in innovative or less orthodox ways. I say that with caution. The Aristotelian and mythic principles behind these tools are true and will outlast all storytellers, but the way that they have been described and handed down to us – with the sometimes rigidness of specifying exactly what page number certain events in a story are to take place – prove only modestly helpful for many of my students and writing friends.

My experience is that students frequently feel frustrated by the obligation to shoehorn their scripts into the strict guidelines of the three acts. Without the models, they feel lost; but working within the models, they feel that their script isn't able to become their unique vision.

When should a screenwriter know to trust these standard tools and when should they not? Additionally, are there any new tools that writers can use for new formats of screen storytelling and to allow for less traditional types of stories to thrive? These questions are at the core of this book.

Writing within the Structural Models

Screenwriting is, more than the act of telling a story, an act of figuring out *how* to tell a story. Such is the purpose of screenwriting models: they aid the writer in telling the best version of a story. Structural models can maximize efficiency and story clarity, and make character arcs more dynamic, among other benefits. They can also help writers figure out what should happen next in the plot by supplying a road map. Models allow the writer to use knowledge and tools gained from generations of earlier writers. Artists and craftspeople are inventors of tools and techniques, which others can then use to help create their own work.

Consider Renaissance painters inventing the practice of depicting perspective on a canvas, and how these techniques became available for others to use this invention to improve their own work. Storytelling tools needed to be invented; to not use that knowledge is akin to wanting to build a car from scratch but ignoring all the prior inventions that would be extremely useful to the enterprise. We build on knowledge. Models – applied correctly to one's writing – show what has worked in the past. Like a long-proven medical treatment with a high percentage of success, models are not guaranteed success, and they will not work in every instance for every writer, but for the struggling writer or the writer looking to improve and tighten the script, using medical jargon, they are clearly indicated.

At the same time, many theories about early dramatic storytelling suggest there is universality to literary models, given the commonalities that myths from a broad range of cultures share in prototypical characters and narrative elements. Whether storytelling – and the ways in which stories are told – is hardwired into the human experience is a tantalizing question. The structure of how stories are told matters greatly to how they are understood, and the emotional and intellectual impact they make on the receivers of the stories. Storytelling models point toward some ancient wellsprings where truth and knowledge exist.

Writing Outside of Structural Models

I have taught these screenwriting models to many undergraduate students, and even when one accepts the above insights, models can still be a hard sell. Much of the resistance I encounter when teaching structure is the students' concern that by following a model, their work will become predictable and less original. Formulaic. That their writing will lose some spark of originality, and somehow bring out cheesy and predictable turns in their stories.

These concerns are valid. A writer should protect with extraordinary vigilance their uniqueness, their idiosyncrasies, and their perspective on storytelling that is – even in small degrees – different from any other writer. And every writer is different from all other writers. Those differences are the seeds of surprise and wonder that we experience when we watch a movie. What separates us from each other is, in fact, a gift. In the thick of writing, when the road is dark, all we really have is our own voice to call out ahead and help us create a path forward.

Structure, applied incorrectly, followed too ardently, or misconstrued, can indeed create formulaic writing. Well-structured writing is very different from formulaic writing – the latter being a sort of bastardization of the former – but it can be hard to parse the difference in the midst of the creative process. A writer might ask themselves how much the structure is helping to guide them through the complexities of a story and how much the model is merely feeding them easy and uninspired solutions. These distinctions can feel muddled when neck-deep in the process.

When these concerns are compiled, many students will reject these models or seek to break "the rules" before they've even given these rules a chance to show how much better they can make the script. Writing without a model can lead to indulgent, confusing writing that wastes precious pages and tends to be boring.

But it would be too easy and unfairly dismissive to say that all of this writing is bad. Much of it brings out the exact things the writers want to protect: nuanced, original writing with strange and wonderful turns. The good is often mucked up with aspects of writing that don't work (that structure would help smooth and improve), but to be sure, something interesting is going on.

Some movies pull it off remarkably well. Spike Jonze's *Being John Malkovich*, John Cassavetes' *Woman Under the Influence*, and David Lynch's *Mulholland Drive* are just a few examples of these masterpieces that shirk, for the most part, classic structural models. Formalists might find a model operating under the hood of these tremendously original films, but it would be a stretch to try and neatly strap the three-act structure around the edges of these wild scripts. One might be able to pull off such a task, but it would be so cumbersome as to likely lose sight of the originality that these films brighten upon the cinematic horizons.

Less structured films can have power in part because their ride is so unpredictable. The structure is like a human's internal clock – you're not always thinking what time it is, but as soon as your attention turns to time, you have a sense of where you are in the day. That sense creates an expectation of pattern for rhythm (it'll be time to eat soon, go to bed soon, etc.). But then you travel somewhere, to a far-flung location away from your time zone, and there's an entirely different feeling afoot. A disorientation that is not unpleasant; a wonderment at trying to get your bearings, which allows you to see the world with more attentiveness and fresher eyes. This is the experience of an unstructured film; you become smaller to the experiences unfolding before you. Those experiences feel bigger and newer. They create deeper memories and experiences, and possible opportunities for new modes of expression.

Less structured films, when well-told, hit audiences differently, perhaps more jarringly and sometimes more interestingly, than films that nail with precision the three-act structure.

Methodology of This Book

The GoFaSt Guide to Screenwriting looks at the question of screenwriting in three parts.

First, the book explores a new structural model, called by its acronym GoFaSt that I developed in my classrooms and through my own writing. It is a model that I feel is more contemporary in its arrangement and allows less orthodox writers to keep their unique voices while providing flexibility to tell their own stories in the most dynamic ways possible. It instructs how to tell a story in a way that students have found to be more freeing, not only of what kinds of stories they want to tell but also of different formats – from movies to episodic series.

Second, the book puts this model to work. I will introduce several storyline ideas in different genres and unfold – in real time, as it were – how the GoFaSt model can be used to develop these concepts into scripts.

Third, the book does the reverse and looks at existing movies – and one episodic show – and uses the model to break down the structures of these stories. Naturally, these scripts were not written using the GoFaSt model; however, by using this method to analyze these stories, we start to notice how cyclical patterns operate within well-told stories. The GoFaSt model is useful for writing one's own scripts, and also for breaking down other scripts to glean the secrets and methods behind their pacing and power.

The GoFaSt Model

One of the driving forces for my developing the GoFaSt model was to combine the seemingly antithetical forces of structured and unstructured writing. The conundrum for the writer is that they must accomplish these two, opposing tasks at the same time (writing freely and writing according to structure) and have those activities work seamlessly together. It can feel like trying to inhale and exhale simultaneously. It can feel impossible. My more flexible model was developed to make this task more feasible.

Another motivation for developing this model is that movies are changing. Indeed, movies have always been changing. Given the new distribution platforms offered by online streaming services, an explosion of audience interest in a wider range of genres and types of stories than ever before, and the greater variety of voices wanting to make films, the change is happening at an accelerated pace. Funding sources for films have broadened, and with the increased number of films being funded, many of these projects are more experimental in form and subject matter. Colloquially put, it's getting wild out there, and writers are looking to break older forms and molds of storytelling and are seeking something other than traditional models to help tell their stories.

While the core fundamentals of drama are steadfast, my goal with the GoFaSt model is to prioritize flexibility for the increasing plurality of types of scripts being written. Trends in storytelling adjust, and the desires of audiences to see stories unfold in different ways adjust, which is why this model remains flexible and doesn't dictate page counts or even the proportion of how many stories should be reserved for set-up versus pay-off.

What is important is letting the writer control the pace and unfolding of the story depending on their unique story's requirements and what is less important is page-count specifics. I'd rather the writer have their hands fully on the steering wheel, and give them a compass setting and let them chart the course that makes sense to them, rather than dictating which road to drive. The GoFaSt model is a compass setting more than a map, and certainly not anything as specific as a beat sheet template. My model trusts the writer to figure out what's best for their own story and to make their own decisions while keeping them going in the correct bearing.

Television and other platforms for screen storytelling are also rapidly developing. The GoFaSt model makes room for television writing and shorter streaming format writing, which the three-act structure and hero's journey do not necessarily accommodate.

Moreover, the GoFaSt model allows the writer to be less linear in how they think about the story and characters. Linearity works for some writers; I have heard of writers who enjoy the step-by-step process of sitting down at page one and writing straight through (over the course of many weeks and months, naturally) until they reach the final page and have a complete draft.

In my experience, this is a rather rare way to write. More often, writers will want to hunt-and-peck their way around the script, growing tired and perhaps frustrated with a certain second-act subplot, and enjoying the novelty of jumping to the third act, before hitting a dead end with that and moving to act one. Round and round they go, working the pages in this instinctive and scattershot approach until the draft is complete.

Linearity can be hard on the writer, as pushing through the pages in sequences can feel like plodding along in an endless marathon – step-by-step-by-step – until numbness and boredom set in. Looking at non-linear – or, at least, less linear – ways of writing can open new connections for the writer, as they jump from page 20, let's say, to page 80, and accidentally happen upon a confluence of ideas, or a mirroring of character behaviors, that is interesting – and that the writer may want to dig in deeper to uncover. It is the equivalent of, for instance, having a messy desk versus a tidy one. The conventional wisdom (which certainly simplifies the issue but is at least illustrative of the point) is that those with messy desks wind up being more creative because a pile of notes from one project will be sitting upon a pile of sketches from another, and perhaps the creative individual will find a connection between these accidental piles to form a new idea. It's the screenwriter's equivalent of the 1970s commercial for Reese's Peanut Butter Cups, where two strangers walking down a street – one carrying chocolate, and one carrying peanut butter – collide, smash their treats together accidentally, and wind up with a snack that improves what each was originally carrying.

Escaping the bonds of linearity can be creatively freeing and put the writer in the enviable position of "happy accidents" – collisions of ideas that had once seemed to exist on separate narrative paths. The GoFaSt model allows the writer to think not only about "what happens next," but to consider all the goals of the characters in the story at once, all the failings at once, or any narrative and character elements in a grouped non-linear way. This is an invigorating and eye-opening experience for a writer, to behold their own writing at a distance, framed in new contexts, to give them fresh eyes on old and worked-over ideas, and to promote new and creative connections.

A Metaphor to Visualize the Model

Goals, failures, and stakes: this is the chain of events that constitutes a single cycle in the GoFaSt model. Each cycle tends to span about twenty to thirty-five pages in a script, and the repetition of these cycles creates a broader structure to the plot.

The protagonist's goals can be visualized as lighthouses set alight in the darkness of the writing experience. This is a metaphor that Robert Towne once used in describing the writing process and is perfectly apt, given how murky and mysterious the journey is to find one's way through a plot. What does the protagonist want? What, specifically, are they trying to achieve? Each of these goals is a lighthouse. A movie only needs a handful to hold together a story – one for each cycle. Once the writer determines the lighthouses (the order or placement of them does not even need to be figured out yet), they will attach a failure to each goal. The more interesting and unexpected the failure, oftentimes, the better the script. (The Coen brothers are masters of delivering deliciously surprising failures to their protagonists. With each failure, their characters become more desperate to succeed, which makes their situations more vulnerable and their subsequent failures more spectacular.) In this metaphor, the failures are the land and rocks built around the lighthouses that keep them upright and support the plot and drama. Finally, bridges are constructed between these land masses, and the bridges constitute the shifts in the stakes of the story that move – with momentum and purpose – the story from one cycle to the next.

If the writer can keep the lighthouses brightly lit, ensure there is enough land built around them so that they do not collapse into insignificance, and keep the bridges clean and strong, then the writers will have the freedom to fill the waters (this can be seen as a theme) and set sail all sorts of ships (characters or subplots) upon those waters as they see fit. Not every element of the script will need to be pinned down to occur on a specific page number, or in a specific order, for the script to work.

Conclusion

This book delivers a model that helps writers write a screenplay. However, this statement should be reconsidered because, in fact, what the writer is doing is *writing a movie*. Writers are not spending their time and talents to merely let their words live forever on a page; they are writing words that will be spoken by actors and describing visuals that will – hopefully – be filmed and seen by audiences. The pages of a screenplay are not akin to the prose of a novel, where the words on the page are both precious and final, and once published, unalterable. A screenplay is a living document meant to change constantly through development, pre-production, and even during production. The words on the page are transient, they are inspiration, and they are designed to lay the foundation for a movie. Few screenwriters have written as evocatively about the craft of screenwriting as the writer/director Christopher McQuarrie.

McQuarrie's career as a screenwriter began when he penned the critical and commercial hit *The Usual Suspects*. In subsequent years, he wrote several big-budget Hollywood actioners, such as the *Mission Impossible* series. McQuarrie's successes in writing led to his becoming the director of, among other films, *Jack Reacher*, starring Tom Cruise.

McQuarrie has written eloquently about many aspects of screenwriting and visual storytelling and has emphasized the importance of prioritizing plot over story. Plot, as he describes it, is information. It is the mechanics of the things that need to happen in a story. But information is not inherently dramatic. Drama comes from questions, not answers; from ambiguity, not information. Mysteries about a character's beliefs or motivations are dramatic. Questions about what a character will do or how they will do something are dramatic. The opaque and complex uncertainties about what a character is feeling or what they might do as a consequence of their feelings are dramatic. These are all in the realm of how McQuarrie defines the story.

If the *plot*, as McQuarrie says, is merely the beats of the screenplay, then the *story* is the emotional journey of a character dreaming of something vital in their lives, being pushed back and hurt and disappointed, and having to recover some semblance of those hopes and dreams – either a tattered version or a version much grander than they initially conceived. Plot is the skeleton. Story is the soul.

The GoFaSt model creates both plot and story but prioritizes story. Plot is necessary because, without it, a character's arc is aimless, and the audience has nothing to grab onto in terms of understanding why the characters are taking the actions that they do. But the story is the most fun part of a movie to watch and – for the writer – the most exciting part to write. Traditional models, when applied too rigidly and without creative flourish from the writer, can usually wind up prioritizing the plot over the story. They are heavy-handed in establishing mechanics over drama.

Remember this most important fact: you are writing a movie. Write your movie with the same abandon and enthusiasm that you experience while watching your favorite films on screen.

References

Cassavetes, John (1974) *A Woman under the Influence*. Faces International.
Jonze, Spike (1999) *Being John Malkovich*. Universal Pictures.
Lynch, David (2001) *Mulholland Drive*. Universal Pictures.
McQuarrie, Christopher (2012) *Jack Reacher*. Paramount Pictures.
Singer, Bryan (1995) *The Usual Suspects*. Tristar Film.

The GoFaSt Guide to Screenwriting

2

GOALS

The Writing Process

Ideas for screenplays originate from mysterious places. Often, the writer will have no idea where an idea came from – it may appear instantly, from seemingly no place at all. Part of the excitement of having a new idea is how rare the moment is since it is unlikely that the writer can continue to return to that same wellspring over and over for more ideas. Andy Warhol once claimed that ideas for his art came from mishearing conversations. Such accidents of inspiration can hardly be called upon at will.

That initial moment when an idea pops into the head of a writer sparkles, as the writer is filled with the limitless potential for how great the movie could be – what the film might look like, the trailer, the poster. But it is difficult to *decide* to have an idea. Try it. Sit down and force yourself to think of a movie idea. It's possible, but often the idea winds up being contrived and not quite as alive or exciting as ideas that come unexpectedly.

So where do these ideas come from?

Perhaps there's a compelling setting – maybe a seaside town or a bustling city – that inspires the writer, and they begin writing to explore the location and its people. Sometimes the idea is taken from a real person's life, and the writing process becomes about structuring existing true events into a narrative. Perhaps limitations on a budget can be the source of an idea for a script (well, if we can only afford three actors and one location, what sort of story could emerge?) A dream, a memory, or a sudden feeling can also spark ideas. Our imaginations are flint constantly hitting against the things we see every day, the people we meet, and the movies we watch, and every now and again, there's a spark.

DOI: 10.4324/9781003141549-2

However, the exuberance a writer feels about having a great, new idea cannot entirely be trusted because every idea – no matter how thrilling – comes embedded with problems that must be eventually solved and slogged through that aren't yet apparent when they're still sparkling so brightly in one's eyes.

This may sound depressing, but in fact, this is the good news: even if coming up with an idea for a script is usually outside of the writer's control, the writing process is mostly within the writer's command. Some days prove to be more productive than others, certainly, and every writer has faced writing days when their mind feels empty and no good work can be accomplished. Nevertheless, there are specific tasks that a writer can endeavor to write each day, and therefore the writer doesn't need to sit around waiting for some great accident of inspiration to occur.

This book is meant to provide a new model for the writer to make that long slog from inspiration to a finished screenplay. This book is not about accidental creativity; it is about the work of creativity. And the model is meant to apply to all, or at least most, genres, types of screen stories, budgets, etc. As lost as a writer becomes, this model directs the writer through the furthest, darkest corners where they can find themselves to steer them toward a productive direction.

However, the process of taking an idea and expanding it into a storyline is as varied as the writers themselves. Everyone does it differently. What is shared amongst all writers is that writing is hard, and what is shared amongst most writers are certain principles of *how* to approach writing. These principles are, essentially, models for how to take an idea and explode that idea into one hundred and ten pages of screenplay. There are many models for screenwriting; some are fashionable and trendy and disappear over time, while others last through the ages, such as the Three Act Structure, laid out in its original conception by Aristotle.

Many writers begin with an outline or by sketching scenes on notecards and arranging them into sequences. This is the equivalent of starting from the outside of the script, creating the borders, as it were, or the shape of the story, and then working one's way into the interior of the story. Alternatively, a writer might dive straight into writing pages of dialogue to discover the characters or the events of the narrative and then work outward to build the script's shape and structure.

There is no absolute right way or wrong way. If the writer is following a path that excites them and progress is being made, then they're probably doing it right. The instinctive propulsions of the creative mind should be followed first and foremost, above all rules or principles of screenwriting and above anyone's dictums or advice about the proper way to write. Indeed, the proper way is the way that feels best to the individual writer on a particular script.

Quite frequently, though, after a long period of writing, the writer will start to accumulate an unwieldy amount of material. Or, alternatively, a writer may struggle to accumulate enough material and find that the gaps between sequences or sections of the script feel like untraversable deserts. Inevitably, the creative output, which sometimes plays out like a fever of writing, leads the writer into a phase where they must begin to think more logically about the narrative – where pacing, character arcs, and proper dramatic pay-offs must be calibrated into a more refined form to improve the script from a wonderful, though messy, idea into something that audiences can experience as a cohesive narrative experience.

The GoFaSt model can be useful for figuring out how to organize a neck-deep pile of notes and thoughts or for trying to stitch together the bare-minimum basics of the storyline.

The GoFaSt Cycle: Phase One

Goals, failures, and stakes: this is the basic structural machinery that drives a character's narrative journey through a script. The character passes through each phase of this cycle – first setting a goal, second experiencing failure in trying to achieve that goal, and third seeing the stakes adjusting as a result of that failure. This cycle happens over and over in the script until the story concludes.

How long is each cycle? Usually about twenty to thirty-five pages. But – as we'll learn in this book – the length of a cycle is far less important than its structural integrity.

How many cycles does it take to finish the story? As many cycles as can fit in the format of the narrative being written.

What differentiates the last cycle from the earlier cycles? The differences are not great, except that the last cycle's failure will have a sense of finality, and instead of a phase of "stakes," there's usually a summation of the "resonance" of the character's journey.

We'll discuss this all in more detail throughout the book. For now, let's become more familiar with the first phase of the cycle: goals.

Some of the most enduring works of narrative drama feature characters trying to achieve a specific goal. Homer's *Odyssey* is about a king trying to return home after the Trojan War. *Hamlet* is about a prince seeking revenge against his uncle. *Frankenstein* is about a scientist trying to help, and then destroy, his monstrous creation. These are stories about someone needing to do something. To get somewhere, to kill someone, to create something. These stories explore profound and complex themes of the human experience. But the narratives themselves are not driven – in terms of plot mechanics – by philosophies, ideas, or cultural commentaries. Those abstractions emerge as a by-product of the core action of a character trying to achieve a goal.

14 Goals

Themes arise when a character takes action, but when a writer is too on-the-nose when writing a theme, the film can feel preachy and didactic.

There is a common concern from writers that plot-driven stories lack complexity or sophistication. Sometimes, a distinction is drawn between plot-driven movies and character-driven movies. This distinction is misleading and can motivate writers to stray away from delivering a strong narrative through-line. Judging by the number of academic dissertations written about *The Odyssey*, *Hamlet*, and *Frankenstein*, it's safe to call those works sophisticated and complex. But they're also plot-driven. In each of them, a character has a singular goal they're trying to achieve.

When screenwriters are concerned about plot-driven stories being "dumbed down," the simplicity of the narrative that they're negatively reacting to is more likely caused by the plodding execution of the plot, not the existence of the plot.

In the first stage of the GoFaSt model, a character has a goal. The most compelling goals have specific qualities that make them especially useful for creating drama or thematic complexity. To understand what makes an effective goal in this model, let's examine the two concepts: *qualities* of goals and *types* of goals.

Qualities of Goals

Actionable

A goal motivates the character to *do* something – to take action. The screenwriter should focus on making these goals tangible and visual. For instance, in *The Odyssey*, a king trying to return home is actionable: he must procure a boat, he must cross a sea, he must defend against threats along the way, he must eat and sleep to survive. An actionable goal means that there are concrete steps the character can take to achieve the goal. These steps – or sequences – provide shape, form, and narrative momentum for subsequent scenes. Each one of those sequences becomes a font of possible scenes and dramatic events, an opportunity for the character to prove themselves, or not. To show weakness, strength, or any qualities that the writer wants to tease out of this character.

Additionally, an actionable goal sets the audience's expectations for the story. In the movie *Good Time*, directed by the Safdie brothers, the initial goal is to rob a bank in Queens, New York. With the introduction of this goal, the audience is now properly on the playing field that the filmmakers have established: this movie is going to be a gritty, urban crime story. Properly set expectations are important to maintain a dramatic world that is cohesive, where certain things are likely to happen and other things are unlikely to happen. For instance, with the brothers' goal of robbing a bank established, the story will follow the steps required for pulling off the heist. They need disguises, possibly weapons, a plan, etc. These all become important elements for creating the bank heist sequence in the film. Subsequently, after the heist, the audience should expect the police to get involved; narrow escapes and loss of life will likely come to bear.

Now, it is important to note that audience expectations do not have to be revered, and the writer is under no obligation to give the audience exactly what they expect; on the contrary, expectations can be treated playfully and experimentally in the hands of the writer. Expectations can be subverted and twisted to keep an audience on its toes and unsure of what *exactly* will happen next. But what happens next usually should take place within the ballfield of the world that the goal has established. If the movie starts in Queens as an urban heist film and winds up in outer space with lightsabers, something might have gone off the rails along the course of the plot. An actionable goal can help keep the story grounded.

Verifiable

Verifiability means that there should be clarity about whether – and when – the protagonist has failed or succeeded at pursuing their goal. If the goal is such that the audience is left unclear about whether or not it has been achieved, then the audience is left in a sort of dramatic limbo, and the script can stall.

Vagueness is a different concept than ambiguity. Ambiguity can be a powerful tool. Take, for instance, an ending that is ambiguous, where there are many different reasonable possibilities for what happens to a character. This can be dramatically exciting, leading the audience to debate "what happened" after the movie has ended. In *Blade Runner*, the question of whether Rick Deckard is a replicant is ambiguous – there are intriguing arguments to be made for and against. Ambiguity often reflects the complex nature of the world, where perspective plays a large role in understanding the circumstances and outcomes of a character.

Vagueness, on the other hand, is an outcome that feels muddy or confusing. Vagueness is frustrating for an audience. If a goal is not verifiable, then it risks being vague.

For instance, if a character's goal in a movie is to be rich, this is probably not verifiable because one person's wealth is measured relative to other people's wealth. A millionaire is rich to someone making the minimum wage, but not to a billionaire. Similarly, happiness is not a verifiable goal for a character. How do you know when someone is happy? Happiness is hard to measure because it is more than just a smile on the face. Happiness usually comes in waves – with people going from being happy to being stressed and then back again with some degree of regularity throughout a day or week.

Happiness exists on a continuum that pendulum-swings over time. So how does the audience know when the character has crossed the finish line?

If the writer wants the character's happiness to be an end-product of the movie, the emotional outcome – happiness – wouldn't be the goal itself. It's better to choose a verifiable goal – let's say, to marry a specific person whom the character has long and secretly loved. Happiness will be an outcome of the goal having been achieved.

Similarly, and perhaps more interestingly, is when the goal proves to be a misguided venture for the character – a fool's errand – and therefore the character needs to realign themselves with a new goal. Perhaps the character thinks that money will be the answer to achieving happiness, so they decide to rob a bank. Robbing a bank is unlikely to lead to happiness, which creates room for the protagonist to do something wonderful: to be wrong. To have to change their mind and adjust their plan. To get into trouble. To have to get out of trouble.

As the writer, have an eye on the desired emotional outcome for the characters, and then consider a verifiable goal that shows them either having failed or having achieved the goal.

Simplicity

Story and character complexity are often best when earned over the course of a movie. A simple goal can lead to unlimited complexity. Complexity is best suited as an outcome of a situation going awry rather than thrusting the audience into a sudden maze of plot circumstances. In *Good Time*, the initial goal is simple: to rob a bank. Same for *There Will Be Blood*, where the initial goal is to strike oil. In the film *Eternal Sunshine of the Spotless Mind*, the protagonist's goal is to forget his girlfriend. Simple goals – all of these. And yet, no one would mistake any of the movies as being simplistic. These are rich, layered films where the complexity arises from the consequences of trying to achieve their otherwise straightforward goals. (This concept will be fleshed out more in the "Failures" chapter in this book.)

Simple goals also reinforce the principle that goals should be actionable and verifiable. The more elaborate or complicated the goal, the harder it may be to know when and if the goal has been achieved. A useful exercise is to try and limit the goal to a single word (money, oil, and forgetting – in the above examples). If the writer can do this, then they find themselves in a solid place to have an effective goal.

Moreover, highly complex goals can leave the audience feeling confused. Confusing the audience isn't – unilaterally – such a bad thing, but confusing an audience at the start of the movie (when the goal is being laid out) can make for a slow start to the film.

Difficulty

The goal should be hard to attain. Struggle is compelling. Writers tend to go too easy on their protagonists. This can be the result of the sympathy that a writer naturally holds for their protagonist, that they don't want them to suffer inordinately. Or sometimes writers haven't fully explored the limitations of what is possible in their scripts; they don't know how far they can push things and therefore may not push far enough.

But without sufficient struggle, embarrassment, or suffering – or combinations therein – the arc of a character's journey can fall flat. Therefore, the goal must be hard. Or, at least, hard for this specific character to accomplish. In the film *Bicycle Thieves*, a father and son must locate a bicycle that was stolen from them. Without the bicycle, the father will lose his job, and the family will go without food. Set in Rome, the goal of finding one stolen bicycle is certainly a difficult one. The task may not be hard for a character like Sherlock Holmes, but for the father in *Bicycle Thieves*, an ordinary man busy with a family and financial struggles, this is notably difficult.

If the goal is not sufficiently challenging, then the audience winds up being in the position of knowing what the character should do before the character does, figuring out a pathway to success before the character can even get there. Letting the audience get ahead of the character is a risky position for a writer. Also, audiences famously appreciate underdogs, and underdogs need to have their work cut out for them, where the chances of success are, by definition, slim. To have failure be the greater chance, the goal must be difficult.

In another example, in the Abbas Kiarostami masterpiece *Where is the Friend's House?*, the protagonist – a child – must deliver a notebook to a classmate who lives in another village. If the notebook is not given, then the classmate will not be able to complete his homework and will be expelled from school. Finding out where someone lives in a small, nearby village is not objectively difficult. But for a child, it is hard. He must travel on foot, query adults whom he does not know, and do various things that are difficult for a slightly shy, introverted child like this protagonist. Consequently, the ensuing drama is profoundly compelling.

Free from Morals

Chalk this up to writers sometimes wanting things too good for their protagonists, but scripts can be undermined if the high moral qualities of the protagonist's goal are meant to be the reason that we like the protagonist. Moral goals do not make better goals – they do not make goals more dramatic, compelling, or vital to the audience's interests. This isn't to say that the protagonist's goal can't be morally good, but a goal doesn't need to be, and the writer should not use this goal to force the audience to like this character.

Such efforts read as a sort of audience pandering and make for a character who is "likeable" only in the most generic and bland way.

In the film *Dog Day Afternoon*, the protagonist Sonny's goal is to rob a bank. Certainly, this is an immoral activity. However, our sympathies for him run deep. Why? Because we understand (later in the film) his motivation. A character's ability to come across as authentic makes them more likeable than a character who is trying to simply do the moral thing. We admire Sonny for how he handles the obstacles, challenges, and failures in attempting to achieve his goal. And – indeed – there are whiffs of goodness in him when he acts sympathetically toward the clerks who need to use the bathroom. Admiration also ties the audience to Walter White in his quest to cook meth in *Breaking Bad*. Eventually, the audience understands that he's making meth to provide for his family – but the joy the audience gets from Walter's escapades comes much less from this reason than the thrill he experiences for breaking the law.

A final note on the importance of non-morality in goals. Goals aren't always what the protagonist actually wants – the goal is only what they *think* they want. The audience only gets to see a character's true colors when the character reacts to the obstacles presented to them. A moral goal (especially one too early in the film) creates a character who perhaps knows too soon what they need in life and limits the potential growth they might have as a character. The goodness often comes out in the arc – perhaps wanting something morally "bad" at first – rather than the moral qualities of the goal itself.

What is most important is determining whether the goal is authentic to the specific qualities of the protagonist – authentic as either an expression of who they really are or authentic as an expression of their misconceptions about themselves or the world. The more personal the goal is, the better, and that's far more important to us liking the characters than anything they might hope to achieve.

Types of Goals

Identifying a protagonist's goal can give shape to the course of the narrative, create space for the character to be expressive and let the audience know them, provide pace and propulsion to the narrative, and inspire dialogue that is driven and *about something*.

This section examines some common types of goals. These are not templates – these are topics. Once a goal is in place, the story and characters can begin to write themselves.

For instance, let's take the example of a movie about a character who wants to find Bigfoot and be able to present him to the world. Perhaps this character saw Bigfoot as a child, spent her life retelling this story and getting ridiculed for it, and now wants to prove that she was right.

What goals might be available for structuring the script? Perhaps she needs to locate a recent sighting of a Bigfoot. That could send her to Internet chat boards for Bigfoot enthusiasts and require her to ingratiate herself with them. Maybe these enthusiasts are protective of their information, so her goal is to gain their trust. Maybe she must go out into the woods with them and show off her outdoor skills. To do this, she'd have to save one of their lives. That's a possible goal.

Another story direction could be that, to find Bigfoot, she must build a cage to capture him. Perhaps she needs special materials or expertise, which would make her goal of finding an elusive cage-maker.

Another story direction could be that she wants to find where she saw Bigfoot as a child. She does not remember where her family was, and so to find this information, she must talk to her father. Let's say they're not on speaking terms, so she must rectify their relationship to get the info.

These are three goals that are all viable and logical extensions of the premise of the film.

Alternatively, a goal will strike a writer as compelling and (more importantly) true for the character, and so the writer works backward from that goal to frame out toward the beginning of the story. Perhaps a writer has an idea in their head: a young woman shows up at her dad's house wanting to reconcile with him. This is a goal. There's something compelling about this goal. Maybe there's a detail that the garden is full of dead flowers and the woman is worried about her father's health. A writer could then work backward from this goal. Why would she need to reconcile with him? Does she want to reconcile for his money? Or, perhaps, to learn the location of a trip many years ago when she spotted Bigfoot.

So let's dive in a bit deeper into these principles and look at five *types of goals* that can be used as diving boards for a writer's task of starting a cycle. Naturally, goals can be combinations of these types. This list is not meant to send the writer into a paint-by-numbers approach to designing or organizing their cycles. Rather, this list is akin to speaking the vocabulary of character goals. The particular use of this vocabulary – the connotative uses of it, as it were – and the arrangement of the words are up to the writer to choose.

A Physical Object

The gold in *Treasure of the Sierra Madre*. The briefcase in *Pulp Fiction*. The cash from *No Country for Old Men*. A physical object – not always a monetary one, but it frequently is – can drive and motivate a character in a way that is deceptively complex. What is interesting about trying to attain a physical object is that it often doesn't require much exposition or justification. For instance, a writer doesn't need to spend time explaining why a character would need a suitcase full of money. The goal of a physical object helps to keep the audience grounded in the succeeding events of the script.

Even more to the advantage of the screenwriter, then, is that the subsequent failures that the character endures in trying to achieve the goal can increase the complexity of the movie while tamping down the confusion. Complexity is wonderful in a script; confusion can only be tolerated by an audience for a short period of time. A complicated goal mixed with complications from the challenges and failures that a character endures could risk being too much for an audience to want to endure. With a compellingly linear goal like a physical object, an entire universe of juicy complications becomes available to the screenwriter.

To Save Someone

In the World War I film *1917*, two British soldiers must race across enemy territory to call off an attack that will kill over a thousand fellow soldiers. In the futuristic movie *Escape from New York*, Manhattan has become an island prison, and a criminal must find and rescue the United States President – who has been trapped on the island – before he's killed.

Goals designed to save someone can shed an altruistic light on a character. However, as previously mentioned, it can be risky for a screenwriter to lean on this altruism as a sign of a character's virtues. In most cases, those virtues should derive from other places in the script (for instance, how well a character handles a stressful situation) rather than the goal itself. And, indeed, for these two examples, these goals don't inherently show the altruism of the characters. In *1917*, the goal is issued by a ranking commander and is therefore not a willful choice by the characters to endeavor to achieve it (although the brotherly connection that one of the protagonists has certainly makes the goal more personal). And in *Escape from New York*, the criminal has no love for the president and is only looking to save himself by saving the president. The goal of saving someone does not need to be openly altruistic, and sometimes, this nuance helps make the characters feel less pandering to the audience and more authentic.

Victory

A boxer wanting to win a match or a soldier fighting to win a battle or war. These are goals where a character is trying to achieve a victory. These goals can sometimes risk being underwhelming once they are achieved. If the audience spends a section of the movie waiting (and expecting) for someone to win a victory, when they do, the victory can feel hollow unless added stakes (we'll get into this section of the cycle) are added to it, or the goal is combined with another goal, such as personal redemption.

Personal Redemption

Goals that feature personal redemption often dovetail with other types of goals. For instance, in *Rocky*, Rocky's attempt to win in the movie's climactic match is an important goal for him. However, the victory ultimately becomes about personal redemption – which is partially the reason why the movie is so satisfying even though he loses the climactic match. A victory in-and-of-itself carries a less dramatic punch than a screenwriter might assume. It's the journey and the stakes that ultimately matter more than the win.

Personal redemption goals can also reflect the inner struggles of a character. For instance, in the drama *Clean and Sober*, Michael Keaton's character plays an alcoholic who finds himself on a journey toward sobriety. The sobriety is his personal redemption and opens up a wide birth of opportunities for a screenwriter to display a significant arc for a character.

Destination

A character needing to get somewhere is the goal of a range of movies, from road films to comedies to thrillers. In *Planes, Trains and Automobiles*, Steve Martin's character is trying to travel home for Thanksgiving. An array of challenges (canceled flights, long distances, and a troublesome cohort) open up to the screenwriter to explore this goal. In *Pulp Fiction*, the character Butch's goal is to leave town after winning a boxing match that he was supposed to lose, killing his opponent in the process. His destination is to escape the town before crime boss Marsellus (who lost money in the boxing match) catches him. Butch's goal is thwarted by a missing watch and a gimp. As in the physical object goal, the linearity of the destination goal is appealingly linear, opening up the story to all kinds of narratively outrageous obstacles.

Conclusion

The goal is the first phase of the GoFaSt cycle. Each cycle will have its own goal that builds off the previous cycle's (undoubtedly) unattained goal – a concept we will explore in the next chapter.

This structural device – where the goals evolve during the narrative – is useful because it looks at the character's journey as less monolithic. It also allows the screenwriter to avoid the notoriously unruly expansiveness of Act Two – the middle of the script – that writers often struggle to fill and give shape to. In the GoFaSt model, there is no middle; there's just a new cycle that refreshes the drama, tightens the character's journey, and keeps the pace of the story moving forward.

Within the context of the Christopher McQuarrie distinction of *plot* vs. *story* discussed in the first chapter, goals are akin to the plot of the story.

22 Goals

They provide information to the audience about why a character is doing something and the mechanics of what will be happening in this movie. Goals are literal, in a certain regard, and while necessary, not enough to hang one's writerly hat on in terms of exciting or enthralling an audience. Goals are the starting gun, but they are not the race. That excitement – that race – and all the delicious *stories* that truly engage an audience come to fruition once the protagonist begins to fail. This concept of failure will be examined in the next chapter.

Study Guide

In elementary school, it is common practice to learn how to diagram a sentence. This sometimes-loved (though often-hated) activity is useful for creating a schematic representation of the grammatical parts of a sentence. When considering the structure of a film and seeking to learn from what it does right, or when rewriting one's own screenplay, creating a schematic visual aid can be equally useful to see what's already there – and what's missing.

As a study guide for this chapter, try this: pick a movie that works particularly well in its pacing and plot. Or, if writing a screenplay, then do this activity with your script. Watch the movie – or re-read your script – and every twenty-to-thirty-five minutes of screen time (or every twenty-to-thirty-five pages), write down the protagonist's goal.

If there are multiple protagonists or if the most important goals in each section of the script change hands from one protagonist to another, make note of this, as well.

Two things to observe as you do this activity:

1) Can the goal be stated in one word (most preferable) or just a few words?
2) How often (at the minute-marker or page number) does the goal change?

Often, a protagonist's goal is thought to be an overarching goal meant to be achieved at the end of the movie. This is not particularly helpful to the writer as they structure a script. To be clear: a protagonist may well have a stated goal that will be paid off at the end of the script, but a few pages into the script, the protagonist will need to take on a series of short-term goals that – ideally and most commonly – will shift and evolve into new, short-term goals throughout the script.

How many goals have you identified in the movie or script? Take a moment to consider how closely they relate to each other. Are they all quite similar or different? Later chapters in this book have examples of goals that can seem very different from one another (read the analysis of *There Will Be Blood*) and goals that seem quite similar from one cycle to the next (read *Portrait of a Lady on Fire*). However, it is likely that the goals should not be the exact same, over and over, from one cycle to the next. If that is the case, then the script or movie might feel repetitive. Goals should – like characters – develop and change during the course of the movie and reflect the increasing complexity of what the protagonist is endeavoring to accomplish.

References

Anderson, Paul Thomas (2007) *There Will Be Blood*. Paramount.
Avildsen, John G. (1976) *Rocky*. United Artists.
Caron, Glenn Gordon (1988) *Clean and Sober*. Warner Bros.
Carpenter, John (1981) *Escape from New York*. AVCO Embassy Pictures.
Coen, Joel and Ethan (2007) *No Country for Old Men*. Miramax Films.
DeSica, Vittorio (1948) *Bicycle Thieves*. Ente Nazionale.
Gondry, Michel (2004) *Eternal Sunshine of the Spotless Mind*. Focus Features.
Homer, *Odyssey*.
Hughes, John (1987) *Planes, Trains and Automobiles*. Paramount PicturesTarantino, Quentin (1994) *Pulp Fiction*. Miramax Films.
Huston, John (1948) *The Treasure of the Sierra Madre*. Warner Bros.
Kiarostami, Abbas (1987) *Where is the Friend's House?* Kanoon.
Lumet, Sidney (1975) *Dog Day Afternoon*. Warner Bros.
Mendes, Sam (2019) *1917*. Dreamworks Pictures.
Safdie, Josh and Benny (2017) *Good Time*. A24.
Scott, Ridley (1982) *Blade Runner*. Warner Bros.
Shakespeare, William *Hamlet*.
Shelley, Mary (1818) *Frankenstein; Or, The Modern Prometheus*.

The GoFaSt Guide to Screenwriting

3
FAILURES

The Nature of Failure

Why do we watch movies? Why occupy ourselves with beating out the crowds of opening weekend moviegoers to buy a ticket to the latest superhero epic? Why chase down rare copies of obscure movies that we haven't seen in years? Why spend an entire day binging the complete season of the latest streaming hit show? As an audience, what are we seeking? What is universal about the experiences offered in such a wide variety of movies, from superhero films to lost cult classics, that attract audiences?

Perhaps audiences watch these stories to be inspired. Or entertained. Or to see reality portrayed on screen. Or to see their worst fears realized before their eyes. Or for an endless myriad of other reasons. Audiences' reasons for watching movies change, as well, depending on their mood, whether they're alone or in a group, and whether they're feeling happy or sad. The reasons are as varied as there are films and shows to experience. And even though no single movie can satisfy all audience's desires, there is one shared characteristic all movies have, that every audience seeks out, and which satisfies a deep, human need: experiencing failure.

Stories become interesting when characters fail. This is not to say that audiences have a masochistic desire to watch misery and heartbreak on screen – quite the opposite, in fact. Nothing quite brings people together in mutual understanding and compassion than the experience of failure, and it is through this shared, empathetic experience that the audience – no matter what they're looking to get from a story – is moved. Roger Ebert once described movies as "empathy-making machines," and the failure dimension of a movie is central to this experience.

In the writer's process of writing a script, failure provides many important functions. Here are two: failures reveal character and move the plot forward. Indeed, the GoFaSt model is designed to drive both plot and character. Failure is instrumental to achieve this.

Plot-driven films *can* be character-driven films when a character's failure feels true and reveals a new dimension of their humanity. It is wise for screenwriters to be stingy with how much success they dole out to their characters. A writer's characters are not their family or friends, so writers shouldn't wish their fictional characters to be happy most of the time. Too much happiness and success for a character not only turns the tone of the film saccharine and unreliable, but it's also dramatically boring because there are not many places for the story to go. Nothing quite rids a person of having a goal than ease and gentle contentment. But even more: without delivering enough failure to the character, the audience will not truly get to know who the character is. For screenwriters interested in developing and fleshing out their characters (and that's probably all screenwriters), keep an eye on the failure section of the GoFaSt model as a place to get to know who your characters are.

Consider the genre of the romantic comedy: set a stopwatch to how many minutes of the movie the couple is together and happy. The total minutes are less than one might expect; the majority of the story is them apart, them at odds, one pining for the oblivious other, or some other combination that creates pain. But the amount of time they've together sticks in the audience's mind because it *means* so much, and the only reason it means that much is because of how much time they spent *not* happily together.

Failures expose a character's weaknesses, thereby illuminating a hidden corner of their personality or past. Have they been disturbed by trauma, or do they suffer from anxiety or depression? From where does their weakness – or vulnerability – derive? To answer that question is to begin the process of creating depth, layering, and complexity in the character.

Failure also shows a character's strength because the audience can see how they recover – in the movie – after facing their weakness. As long as there is another cycle in the story, the character will have taken an action, or made a choice, to create a new goal – and that action or choice, in the face of defeat, shows strength. In this way, failure is what leads the audience to truly know a character, and it allows the screenwriter a narrative upon which to express those qualities to the audience. To showcase those qualities. To explore and explain: *this* is who this character is at their worst, and at their best.

Ultimately, this is also what creates the audience's empathy for a character. Evolutionary research suggests how – as a species – we are more sensitive to failure than success. For early humans, a traumatic attack from an animal can cause a lifetime of fear, because it is the fear that keeps us alive. Fear is perhaps the most powerful of all emotions because it is the one that keeps us the safest. Fear and failure are necessary for survival, and as social beings, we are wired to feel empathy for those experiencing fears and failures. Success can encourage egos and a sense of superiority over others, widen the chasm of class differences among a population, and encourage feelings of jealousy and resentment in those who do not enjoy the same amount of success. But failure has a way of stripping all those things away, leaving us humbled and – often – more desirous of the social connections and mutual emotional understanding of those around us. Failure can leave us in a purer state of oneness with our humanity and those around us. It is a great equalizer.

A screenwriter who wants to make the audience root for a character should find a better place than a goal to get an audience to root for a character – we can pat someone on the back for trying to achieve something hard, but we'll feel deep emotions when we see them struggle and fail, and experience fear and pain when they don't achieve it.

Furthermore, we'll feel admiration when we see them try again.

The GoFaSt Cycle: Phase Two

The character begins each cycle trying to achieve a goal, and – inevitably – they fail to achieve it. Now, failure – for our purposes in this book – is used broadly. Failure may mean that the character doesn't achieve the goal in any way, shape or form. For instance, perhaps the goal for a character was to win a gold medal at a swim meet and, instead, they've come in last place. That is an unquestionable failure.

But failure comes in many varieties. In the GoFaSt model, failure could also mean that the goal was only partially attained, and whatever level of achievement they had, the outcome couldn't be called a success. For instance, in our example, perhaps the character wins the gold medal at the swim meet but then realizes that their primary, and heavily favored, nemesis was sick and didn't compete that day. The character may have won, but with the fans, coaches, and other swimmers assuming that the victory was only because the nemesis didn't compete, the success isn't a true success, and the character remains in a position of having to prove themselves. This would also count as a failure in the GoFaSt model.

Additionally, the character may succeed at the goal, but this success comes at an unexpectedly large and grievous cost. Perhaps a terrible injury has been incurred or something important has been lost in the process of attaining success. Once again, in our example, perhaps the character wins the swim meet and beats the nemesis as well, but in the final stroke to the finish, they rip a shoulder tendon. Success means that now a long and difficult new path (recovery, therapy, and an uncertain future) must be endeavored.

Regardless of how the character's failure comes about, the failure gives a critical time to better understand the character, create a surprise moment or pivot in the plot, and develop the arc of the story.

Failure creates a response in the character; that is, they now must take action. Action creates character. Character is not defined by a list of attributes; rather, a character is someone in motion, making a choice, or reacting in a specific manner. Character – in the dramatic form, at least – is not some abstract notion of who a person is or who we want a person to be. Personality reveals itself when a character moves toward a desire. One's moral compass is revealed only when morals are put to the test in a critical situation. As soon as characters are in motion, they exist. Once they stop, they fade and disappear as characters – or just become extremely boring. A character taking a strong moral stance is fantastic fodder for a movie trailer and will deliver an excellent scene or two, but to truly hook the audience and keep them engaged for the long haul of a fleshed-out narrative, the audience must see a character faltering, failing, reacting, and pivoting, and failing again. The cycles keep them interesting, keep them evolving.

Stories are, at their essence, changes motivated by events. Change gives vibrancy and life to the story, and change only happens when events force that change to happen. But change is hard – in real life, change can be hard to accept, and in stories, change can be difficult to map and describe in an organic and well-paced way. In both cases, failures are necessary for the change. When life is going great, people tend not to want to rock the boat and change their lives – why change when nothing is wrong? In a screenplay, something needs to go wrong.

In the GoFaSt model, each cycle gives the characters an opportunity to react to the failure and, consequently, chart a new course toward a goal. Over the course of the narrative, the cycles show a broader development and growth in the character. For instance, in the first cycle, when the character encounters a failure, what is their response? Self-pity? Defeatism? This response is up to the writer to decide. Then, in the next cycle, when a new failure happens, how does the character respond this time? With resolve? With calm? Depending on the response that the character has to failure, the audience begins to track their arc, where they're starting, and where they're going as a character.

The cycles also give the writer something specific to write about. Thinking about a different response from one cycle to the next can give the writer a sense of how to craft the scenes – a clear purpose for why they're choosing to have the character react one way or another. It gives the writer a *raison d'etre* for their choices.

Failures are exciting to write about. They are like the villains of the structural model world – juicy and delightfully angst-ridden. Goals clarify things;

Qualities of Failures

Resonant

Failure should not be an easy pill to swallow for a character. Simply put, it's got to hurt. Or, as is often the case in comedies, whatever the failure is, it should be very embarrassing. If we think about stories as change, and the failure is the catalyst for that change – and, further, given that human nature generally makes us reluctant to *want* to change – then the failure needs to be resonant.

In the Kelly Reichardt drama *Wendy and Lucy*, a young woman is traveling across the country in search of employment at an Alaska fishery. When she stops in a town in Oregon, her attempts to steal food for her dog land her in jail. When she gets out of jail, she discovers that her dog has gone missing. For such an intimate drama, these are profound failures.

Resonant failures lead the character to rethink their goal or the world around them. The more deeply that the character feels the failure, the more deeply the audience will likely feel for that character.

But here is a caveat: screenwriters should be wary of manipulating the audience's feelings by simply piling hardships onto a character. A screenwriter should not be reckless with an audience's capacity or willingness to sympathize with a character. Sometimes, a big, awful, unlucky event befalls our character, and the failure that they suffer is patently unfair. But other times, the failure emerges from a flaw in the character that, to some degree, their undoing is their own fault – or a sign of weakness – that must be overcome. It is important that the screenwriter is aware of balancing the causes of the failures. How much of it comes from the world being an unfair place, and how much of it comes from the character's own doing?

As in life, the answer is frequently a mixture of both things, and this is an important balance to reflect in one's script.

Unexpected

Think of it this way: if goals are like playing musical standards, then failures are playing the minor keys. Failures are an opportunity for screenwriters to bring a new flair to the script – an unexpected wit and excitement to the story. The films of the Coen brothers are particularly strong examples of how to make a character's failures both devastating and entertaining. Their films begin with characters whose goals start off as rather straightforward (if a bit extreme). In *No Country for Old Men*, the character Llewelyn Moss initiates the plot by trying to bring water to a dying man (and to grab the loot leftover from a shoot-out). In their early comedy, *Raising Arizona*, newlyweds H.I. and Ed are trying to steal a baby.

The subsequent failures are deliciously haywire. In the case of *No Country*, a clean getaway is foiled by a ferocious dog that proves to be a remarkably good swimmer and a gun-toting collector who bets on people's lives with the flip of a coin. In *Raising Arizona*, the newlyweds' goals are undone by escaped convicts who have emerged from a hole in the ground and need a place to hide, and a motorcycle-riding bounty hunter.

The more unexpected the circumstances of the failures (which can occur in how the goal falls through, or in the characterizations of the antagonists, among other possibilities), then the more resourceful the character must be to fix what has happened. If the failure is particularly extreme (while managing to still make sense within the basic ground rules of the film), then the characters must act in equally extreme ways to repair those failures, which puts the screenwriter in a favorable position to write exciting and unexpected material.

Complicating

Goals are useful for being able to simplify the story; failures add complexity. Goals send the narrative forward in a specific, actionable direction; failures are meant to break apart that hyper-directionality. Failures should leave the audience scratching their heads, and an array of possibilities is now opening for the audience to consider what's next. Indeed, the pathway to the next step becomes full of complicated *what-ifs* and *what-nows*.

In the heist drama *Dog Day Afternoon*, the initial goal is to steal money from a bank. But once the pair of robbers are discovered, and police arrive on the scene, a complex set of possible reactions opens up, which the robbers consider: they could barricade themselves, make a daring escape in a helicopter, negotiate their freedom, or start shooting hostages as a show of force. They could choose a path of peace to placate the police or choose a path of force and battle against them. The variety of possibilities from this failure brings to light the various qualities of these characters: scared (barricading themselves), bold (a helicopter escape), and potentially violent (shooting hostages). As we see their personal qualities fan out and the plot reveals its folds and bends, the film becomes a complete experience of fears and laughs, until a new goal is created and the cycles continue.

The writer can then sketch out these various paths – or responses to the failures – and see which one leads to the most fertile creative territory for the next GoFaSt cycle.

New Story Elements

In *Wall-E*, the heroes must deliver a fragile sprout to the spaceship's computer, to alert the ship's command that Earth has, once again, become habitable. Their failure leads to a sequence that sees them being hurtled out into space and nearly destroyed. In *Dog Day Afternoon*, the failure to negotiate an escape leads to the introduction of a new antagonist: an FBI agent who is much more menacing than the police officer with whom the robbers had been dealing.

Alongside the concept of adding complexity, failures offer the screenwriter an opportunity to add new elements to the script. This could be a new character, theme, setting, or idea. Traditionally, the first act of the script is viewed as the most common window for introducing new, major characters or ideas. But this notion can be limiting to the screenwriter, and plenty of great films have seen new characters get introduced halfway or even later in the script. The bigger the window of opportunity that the screenwriter has for organically and convincingly introducing new elements into the script, the more creative storytelling opportunities they have available to them.

The GoFaSt model sees each cycle as a place where these elements can come fresh into the story in ways that won't distract the audience or make these new elements feel contrived or overly plotted.

Types of Failures

Physically Stopped

One of the more common types of failure is when the character is trapped, physically slowed, or prevented from attaining the goal. Perhaps this is a runner losing a race or a wrongfully accused protagonist getting arrested and jailed. In John Cassavetes' *A Woman Under the Influence*, this type of failure is used for several different characters over several cycles of the film. Early in the story, a husband and wife have been planning for an overnight date without their children home. But the husband – Nick – must cancel the date at the last minute when a water main break in the city of Los Angeles (Nick works for the city) forces him to stay on the job and work all through the night. Being forced to stay at work falls under the failure of being physically stopped.

The natural world can also prevent the character from achieving their goal, such as the snowstorm that stops Wendy in her attempts to escape The Overlook Hotel in *The Shining*. In *Cast Away*, the character Chuck Noland survives an airplane crash and winds up alone on a deserted island in the Pacific Ocean. He is stymied by nature and geography in his attempts to escape the island and return to civilization.

Loss of an Important Possession

In *Pulp Fiction*, when a boxer wins a match that he had previously agreed to lose and has now angered a dangerous mob boss, the boxer attempts to flee town with his girlfriend. However, in the rush of packing his things, his prized watch – a family heirloom with a rather distinctive provenance – winds up left behind. This failure leads to a series of misadventures as he attempts to regain possession of the watch, including – rather notoriously – a wild run-in with a pawn shop owner and a leather-clad misfit.

A character losing something vital is a compelling motivator for putting them on an actionable, verifiable journey to recover the lost item. In this example, the film painstakingly explains the importance of the watch to the boxer, and this explanation adds drama to his efforts – the audience acutely understands why he goes to such tremendous lengths to get the watch.

Self-destruction

Most types of failure are external, in that a force beyond the character's control is preventing them from achieving their goal. But sometimes the failure is internal: for instance, a lapsing alcoholic in *Leaving Las Vegas*, or a worn and exhausted Rocky Balboa in *Rocky* losing his "eye of the tiger." A character can be their own worst enemy and allow self-destructiveness to creep in, or doubt that will see them give up the goal in one way or another. Surrender, self-doubt, mental illness, and addiction are all failures that characters can experience. The subsequent cycle often procures a revelation, or new element, for the protagonist that allows them to regain their drive, well-being, or motivation.

This type of failure is intrinsically internal. Film, being a visual medium, thrives when the lives of a screenwriter's characters are expressed externally. Internal angst can, of course, be rendered powerfully on the screen – but the writer should be aware that this kind of failure risks being less cinematic, and therefore the internal self-destruction failures should have outcomes that lead to the external, on-screen action. In the above two examples, the central character's alcoholism causes him to move to Las Vegas (which is a cinematic playground with its flashing lights and bustling street life), and Rocky's loss of motivation leads to visceral, legendary scenes of him training to re-ignite his motivation.

Outsmarted

This failure is akin to being physically stopped but is an intellectual stoppage, or the character losing in a story of gamesmanship or trickery. Spy stories, thrillers, and mysteries – such as the whodunnit *Knives Out* – all use some degree of outsmarting of a character to create a failure.

This type of failure can be particularly thrilling for an audience because it puts the audience in a position of having to guess – along with the character – about the state of what's going on in the story. If the character has been outsmarted, then very likely the audience has as well. Whenever the screenwriter can put themselves ahead of the audience in the knowledge game of a script without hopelessly confusing the audience, very often this works in the screenwriter's favor.

Conclusion

The failure of the protagonist to achieve their goal is a key moment in becoming more deeply human and empathetic to the audience. This failure should not be played to make the audience pity the character – pity is a more superficial reaction to seeing a character going through a rough patch in life, and feelings of pity do not endure for very long. Certainly not for the length of a feature film. Empathy is the deeper, more complex, durable, and lasting emotion that the audience should feel toward the character. True empathy is not forged by the audience feeling bad for the character – rather, empathy occurs when the audience watches a character fall down a rung in the ladder of life, and we can all acknowledge that we've been in that situation, too, felt those same feelings, and that we're all in the same boat as humans living in a complex and uncertain world.

When people talk about "character arc," sometimes writers misunderstand that concept as making sure the characters learn a lesson. If a character learns a lesson, then they have grown wiser, and that will be their change. For instance: instead of a character wanting to merely get rich at the beginning of a movie, they have *learned the lesson* that happiness is more important than money, and this realization will make them better and act differently.

This might be true, but movies that rely on characters changing because they have learned a lesson can often feel pandering. Or simplistic. In real life, people change constantly – in big ways and small ways – but those changes can't always be neatly summarized as a lesson that was learned. Rather, experience is what does most of the changing for a person, especially experiences around failure. Change is hard and uncomfortable. Humans are hard-wired to travel the path of least resistance in life, which is why habits form so easily. Change is the opposite of the ease of forming, or executing, habits; change takes energy and involves risk and sacrifice.

When thinking about your character's arc, think less about a neat lesson they have learned during the movie and think more about the specific experience of the failure that you made them endure – and how they might now behave differently in life because of the sting of that failure. Think less about them *learning* and more about them *experiencing*. This shift in thinking will give your character a more realistic and meaningful arc.

It is important, as the writer, to be flexible on what change looks like in your protagonist. For instance, in *Ferris Bueller's Day Off*, the character Ferris experiences several cycles of goals and failures. However, it would be difficult to describe how Ferris grows as a character; he finishes the movie more-or-less very similar to how he began: playfully irresponsible, impulsive, and prone to not taking life too seriously. Ferris is such an entertaining character that it is doubtful audiences would even want to see him become someone different. And yet, stories – generally speaking – beg for change to feel satisfying; this is not always true for every story, but it is mostly true. So where does the change occur in *Ferris Bueller*? In Ferris's best friend Cameron. As a result of the events of the movie, Cameron grows into a more self-confident character; in terms of screenwriting fundamentals, Cameron changes to that Ferris does not have to.

Another example of how change can be flexibly applied to a script is *Pulp Fiction*. The character of Vincent Vega does not change much, if at all, from the beginning of the movie to the end. He learns no lessons and shows no growth. However, what the audience gets in lieu of change is getting to know Vega. Each scene shows new facets of his character – the audience gets to learn more about how he thinks, what he fears, and who he is. Vega does not change during the movie, but the audience's ideas about him certainly do. And in terms of scratching that "character arc" itch that can sometimes make a script feel formulaic, this different approach is a clever, unusual, and entirely satisfying solution for a screenwriter to use.

Study Guide

The last chapter's Study Guide suggested the activity of writing down the goals that the protagonist has in twenty-to-thirty-five page (or minute) segments in a given movie or screenplay. Let's do a similar diagramming exercise with failures. Each time the protagonist encounters a failure, make a note of what the failure is and the protagonist's response to that failure. Do they try to achieve the same goal in a different way? Do they try to achieve a different, but related, goal?

As discussed in this chapter, failures are a particularly interesting part of a screenplay because that's where most of the surprises and meaty character work exist. Imagine the first goal of your protagonist as being how they want their life to be – or at least this period in their life. The goal represents what is supposed to happen in their lives. However, a life that goes according to plan is probably not a very interesting life. It may feel safe and comforting, but these are not qualities that make for much drama – and certainly not the attributes one would want for a movie. Movies and life are much more interesting when they are unpredictable, and characters and people are richer in character and complexity when they face adversity.

Keeping this philosophy in mind, let's add another element to the diagramming. For each failure, in addition to noting the type of failure and response, do this: write any new attributes you can attach to the protagonist based on their response to their failure.

What has the protagonist's response to their failure taught you – as the viewer of the screenwriter – about the protagonist's deeper character? Alternatively, what has the protagonist learned, or how have they changed, because of the failure? Are they more skeptical, more hardened, more clever, or more broken? Has their worldview, or priorities, as a response to either failing to achieve their goal or having achieved their goal and paid a particularly painful price for the achievement?

If you are revising or working on your screenplay, as you diagram the protagonist's failures, think about having as wide a variety of *types* of failures as possible. It is less interesting and somewhat predictable, naturally, if the protagonist keeps failing due to the same cause or in the same way each cycle. Looking at the list of types of failures in this chapter, look for new ways that the protagonist's efforts can be undone. Use the list or come up with a new idea.

References

Cassavetes, John (1974) *A Woman Under the Influence*. Faces International.
Coen, Joel and Ethan (1987) *Raising Arizona*. 20th Century Fox.
Coen, Joel and Ethan (2007) *No Country for Old Men*. Miramax Films.
Figgis, Mike (1995) *Leaving Las Vegas*. United Artists.
Hughes, John (1986) *Ferris Bueller's Day Off*. Paramount Pictures.
Kubrick, Stanley (1980) *The Shining*. Warner Bros.
Lumet, Sidney (1975) *Dog Day Afternoon*. Warner Bros.
Reichardt, Kelly (2008) *Wendy and Lucy*. Oscilloscope Pictures.
Stanton, Andrew (2008) *Wall-E*. Walt Disney Studios.
Tarantino, Quentin (1994) *Pulp Fiction*. Miramax Films.
Zemeckis, Robert (2000) *Cast Away*. 20th Century Fox.

The GoFaSt Guide to Screenwriting

4
STAKES

Why Stakes Matter

What happens if the protagonist does not achieve their goal? What consequences will they face as a result of encountering failure? If there are no consequences, then does the failure matter? Herein is the topic for this chapter: making failure matter.

Let's say there is a poker player in a Las Vegas casino trying her hand against a table full of other players. A bold but novice player, she is going up against a cadre of hardened professional gamblers with the goal of winning a pot of money. Despite her best efforts and some clever poker plays, she loses several hands in a row. Do we, as the audience, care about this failure? Perhaps we do – but only to a point. Maybe her boldness and ambition win our sympathies, and these qualities alone endear the audience to her, and they root for her success. If she loses, the audience will likely feel bad for her. But audiences don't watch movies and shows to merely be *sympathetic* to a character or to simply feel *bad* for them if they fail. Audiences want to feel much deeper emotions – they want to *love* and *adore* a character and be *devastated* when they fail. A character's charms – as in real life – only go so far in terms of creating an emotional attachment. Giving consequences for the failure embellishes this attachment and makes the events of the story mean more. Consequences add dimension and significance. They also give the story somewhere new to go. If the poker player is merely losing her hands, what's to keep her from just trying again and again and again? How can the audience continue to care?

The answer is, there must be *stakes* in the failure. Let's say that the poker player has come to Vegas to win rent money. If she loses and can't pay her

DOI: 10.4324/9781003141549-4

rent, then she might wind up temporarily homeless. Having come to an unfamiliar city, she may have no one who can offer a couch for her to sleep on at night. She can no longer lose innumerable times; there is now a hard deadline for her. Perhaps she only has enough money to play one hand. A great deal of pressure mounts, then, and this scene of her single hand of poker is going to matter greatly to her – and to the audience.

There is, as an example, a Hollywood thriller from a few years back about a man who had to save his family from a ruthless and deadly gang while working overseas. Saving one's family from murder certainly counts as big stakes. And yet, the film nevertheless ran out of steam about halfway through the story, as he dragged his family here and there trying to escape the gang. One of the reasons was, the stakes did not change. His family's safety was at stake from the first act of the film and did not change even until the end. Even the most important thing in the world to this character – the safety of his wife and children's family – could not sustain ninety minutes of screen time.

How Stakes Enrich a Story

Failures, in the context of the previous chapter, have a universal quality that draws the interest of all audiences, whether they're looking for a dark and dramatic New Hollywood movie from the 1970s or a contemporary light-hearted romantic comedy. The third and last phase of the GoFaSt cycle personalizes the journey of the character by looking at the *stakes*, or consequences of the failure upon the character.

Unlike prose or poetry, which allow the reader to experience the internal territory of a character directly through the author's writings, screen storytelling must access the character's internal workings through an external process: pictures. Since thoughts and feelings cannot be directly photographed – though they can be directly described in, for instance, a novel – the screenwriter must use an outside-in approach to bringing the audience into the emotions and thoughts of a character. That is, through a sequence of images, the audience begins to understand – or, more accurately, *feel* – what a character feels.

Yes, there are exceptions. Voice-over can describe how a character feels, and music and subjective photography can also convey how a character feels. Sad music played over a character looking sad indicates to the audience that, well, this character is sad. However, there is plenty of skepticism about such emotionally on-the-nose use of music, which can simplify a movie and produce feelings that are more pandering than true.

But an entire film or show would be hard-pressed to rely on these techniques exclusively through the narrative. These subjective techniques can be used occasionally, but they are not used *all the time*. Often, a more objective visual strategy is used to piece together a scene so that an audience can make conventionally more sense of what they're watching.

Overly internal films tend to work against the grain of what visual storytelling inherently is: an external medium. And it is important for screenwriters to, for the most part, keep their characters integrated into the broader world beyond just their internal thoughts and feelings. Another way to say this is, the plot saves movies – even character-driven movies – from becoming too internal.

This is one of the key functions of the stakes phase of the GoFaSt model. Goals are specific (they indicate what a character wants in their mind or heart), and failure is usually the result of the person hitting the cold, hard facts of the real world. A character may want that bag of cash, but the security guards, mobsters, or other guardians won't let the character have it. Stakes serve to link the personal with the broader world. What is the movie *saying* about the human condition, or the state of the world, that the character has a hard time getting that bag of cash? Stakes explain – to a degree – a world view about what this all means for the character and for the audience.

Another way to look at stakes is as the consequences of the character's failing. Rent will go unpaid and the character will be evicted from their apartment. Children will go hungry. Imprisonment, illness, or death could also occur – depending on what the character was trying to achieve. These could all be the fates that befall a character who does not achieve their goal.

Stakes enrich a screenplay in other ways, too. Here are a few:

Stakes give us a glimpse into the soul of a character. Understanding *why* someone is doing something in life gives us a glimpse into their deeper qualities as individuals. People's reasons for their actions can be mysterious. Understanding what is at stake to that character brings the audience into, at least, some of the sphere of that mystery. Why do they want the thing that they are risking to attain? What does wanting *that thing* say about who they are?

Stakes also change the shape and size of the story. Phase one of the GoFaSt cycle gives drive to the story. Phase two adds complications to the story. Phase three makes the story dynamic. This is important because, without dynamic shifts in the size and scope of the story, the narrative risks becoming linear and repetitive. There is no single stake that is so important as to be able to sustain an entire film and keep it interesting for the audience. No matter how important that stake is, how big or how dire, what excites and engages audiences are the shifts in the stakes – not necessarily the stake itself.

Stakes must evolve during the narrative. The conventional understanding of how stakes should change, according to the tenets of script development, is that they should grow in scope. For instance, in *Wall-E*, the stakes early in the film are over Wall-E's relationship with Eve, but by the end of the film, the stakes are about the successful re-population of Earth. This is a classical view on the development of stakes and, as in the case of *Wall-E*, work fantastically well.

However, stakes can also grow more intimate. In the film *Dog Day Afternoon*, which opens with an attempted bank robbery, the stakes start quite high: bank robber Sonny's life is at stake as many dozens of police officers swarm the block and guns are pointed into the bank. As the story progresses, though, the narrative shifts to explore Sonny's relationship with a transgender woman, and the stakes become about their relationship. In an objective sense, the stakes become smaller, shifting from a large-scale robbery and police response that involve several city blocks and the safety of many people to a romantic relationship between two people. These stakes are more intimate, and while death is not at stake in the relationship – just love and heartbreak – these new stakes are powerful and fully absorbing and feel "big" even though they're comparatively small to the dozens of police aiming their guns at Sonny.

It should be said that Sonny's risk of death remains an important stake during this later section of the film as well. It is somewhat on the back burner – though still there. This underlines an important observation about stakes that unlike goals (which do best when they are about a single thing), there can be many stakes at once.

So the size of the stakes is far less important – and even not important at all – compared to how those stakes are rendered, and how emotionally invested the audience is. Essentially, regardless of whether they're big or small, *do the stakes matter?* In the film *Wendy and Lucy*, a young woman loses her dog in a small, unfamiliar town, and she must find the animal. A lost dog is traumatizing, but compared to the earlier example of the unsatisfying Hollywood thriller, not as big as one's wife and children being killed. However, *Wendy and Lucy*'s stakes feel much more emotional. The more human rendering in *Wendy and Lucy*, deep character work, and shifting stakes (it's her road trip that is at stake, initially in the film), mean that a lost dog hits emotionally far harder. The same can be said of other films with supposedly small stakes, such as *Bicycle Thieves* and *Where is the Friend's House?*

Let's touch on one last thought on stakes and how stakes relate to a theme before moving on to the more nuts-and-bolts explanation for how stakes can be applied in the GoFaSt model. The theme is a secret sauce that can elevate a script beyond its composite parts of structure, dialogue, and character. It is not an uncommon experience to read a script that is structurally sound and correctly written in terms of pacing and the other vital elements of screenwriting but feel that "something is missing." It can be hard to put one's finger on it. When that happens, often the theme is weak.

What is theme? There is a misunderstanding of the theme that it is a type of "lesson" that the movie is trying to impart to the audience. Family is more important than money. Beauty is more than skin deep. These are cliches that are sometimes passed off as themes. For an audience member, the opportunity to re-learn the tired (although admittedly true) lesson that beauty is more than skin deep, seems a very poor reason to pay the price of admission for a film.

Theme, properly applied, is a more abstract and powerful tool than this. Theme can be a philosophy that runs through the story or a larger question that is examined through the story and its characters but not necessarily answered. Think about the theme of family in *There Will Be Blood*, where the film makes no pronouncements on family being more important than money or any other such tripe trope but instead examines the pain and challenges of what happens when family and money collide. Imagine a jeweler holding up a gem to the light and turning it, noticing how the light hits it in a variety of ways. This is akin to how a script can use theme – by exploring a topic rather than reducing it to a bumper sticker slogan.

Screenwriters should be wary of being too on-to-the-nose about a theme. They should be aware of it as they write, but trouble (corniness, for instance) can occur when a writer writes about the theme too directly. Theme can be thought of as the dark matter in the universe – something mysterious that is impossible to see, but whose gravitational pull is what holds together all the stars, planets, and gasses. Or, in our own particular universe of screenwriting, the theme is what holds together the story elements.

The notion of stakes can help a writer grasp and contend with the slippery issues of the theme. In *There Will Be Blood*, family is at stake. Money is at stake. Considering what is at stake for a character is often a matter of theme because – as discussed – the stakes are a *why* question for the character. Why are they trying to achieve their goal? What does it say about their priorities in life, their principles, and what matters to them?

The three phases of the GoFaSt model explore more than just the structural elements of screenwriting. Understanding the goal phase helps the screenwriter write meaningful and purposeful dialogue. Understanding the failure phase helps the screenwriter better develop the complexities of the character. And, finally, understanding the stakes helps the screenwriter coalesce the themes of the script.

Let's look now at the stakes within the sequence of these three phases.

The GoFaSt Cycle: Phase Three

Stakes are the final phase in the GoFaSt Cycle and change with each cycle. There will be several such cycles in a single narrative. How many cycles depend on the length of the script and the length of each cycle. This model offers flexibility in that regard – what is less important is a specific action happening on a certain page in the script; what is more important is that each phase of the cycle is proficiently written before the next cycle completes.

With each new goal (in each cycle) that the protagonist attempts, something new is at risk. The stake is what the character risks losing from failure. Phase one provides them a goal, phase two enchants the character with some version of failure, and phase three provides the impetus for beginning the next cycle. This third phase gives a new *why* for the character to set out and attempt to achieve a new goal in the next cycle.

Phase three can be thought of as the segue, or reason, for the character to enter the next GoFaSt cycle. Once a goal is failed, the character won't simply enter a new goal unless there's a reason for them to do so. Without a reason driving a new goal, the narrative may feel more like a collection of stories about the character rather than a cohesive narrative that builds with a singular emotional and dramatic crescendo. If, by failing to acquire some item in one cycle, the stakes may be that they have lost the trust of a friend; the next cycle will see the character set about a new goal to regain that trust. But by orienting the next goal around this new stake, the audience has an opportunity to gain insight into the deeper qualities of the character or themes that are important. If the desire to gain the trust of a friend is what motivates the new cycle, then we have learned something important about who this character is. Even if their actions are immoral to achieve the goal, the audience understands the *why* of their actions which lets us see the humanity in them and allows us to feel connected to the character.

The final cycle of a narrative determines whether the film has a happier or more tragic ending. If the character can achieve not just the goal – but what is at stake – in the ending, then the narrative finishes with a character who is not only triumphant but also fulfilled. Alternatively, if whatever is at stake in the end is not achieved, then not only has the character failed at the goal, but their loss resonates as a deep sense of unfulfillment. The final stakes give resonance, weight, and emotional depth to the final account of whether the character achieved or failed at their final goal.

It also allows the filmmaker to convey a sense of a worldview about life, not in a preachy and didactic way but on the level of emotion, where one's general perspective on the world as being a scary, wonderful, dangerous, or loving place (based on how the character winds up at the end of this final cycle).

Qualities of Stakes

Meaningful

If the stakes do not matter to the character, then their endeavors will not matter to the audience. The character must care about losing what's at stake to not only motivate them to want to achieve the goal but also to inspire the audience to worry and root for them throughout the journey.

It is important that stakes not be generic. Money is generally important to everyone, but this doesn't mean that putting money at risk is necessarily going to be an effective stake. Stakes work best when they are specifically meaningful to the main character. What is the writer saying about this character that *this* stake is the thing about which they're most worried to lose? What is the character's personal connection to what's at stake? What does it say about them, their history, their ambitions, or their fears?

Because stakes can be an opportunity to show a nuanced undercurrent of who the character is, their deeper morality or personality, the writer is *saying something* about the character. Be sure it counts.

Finite

Related to the above topic, whatever is at stake must be a finite resource. The thing that the character risks losing of limited supply, and therefore worth preserving. Someone's life at stake makes sense. Presuming certain natural laws of the universe, we all only have one life to live – this is certainly an extremely finite resource. Money is finite, making it a common object to be at risk for a character, provided that their pursuit of money has some specific purpose in the character's life. More esoteric items such as one's reputation and the love from a spouse can also be finite, and therefore those are things well worth protecting and would be very dire for a character to lose.

Layered

Goals thrive by being simple, linear, and straightforward. Stakes are an opportunity for the writer to build additional complexity and nuance into the characterization. Looking back at the earlier example of money being at stake, in the film *Uncut Gems*, Howard risks losing money, but the stake is layered into something more vital: his desire to win, to destroy his competition, and – like a professional athlete – this motivation to feel like a winner defines him.

The more tethers that connect the character to the stakes, and the deeper those tethers reach and connect beneath the skin and attach to their identity, the more the events of the narrative matter to the character – and the more the movie matters to the audience.

Types of Stakes

One's Well-Being

There are few things more meaningful, finite, and layered in importance than one's own life or well-being. Avoiding physical peril is a very common type of stake and with reason. Preserving one's life is not usually viewed as a selfish quality in a character (unless it's at the expense of others' lives), and therefore stakes such as death, injury, imprisonment, and the like, are commonly effective stakes.

Others' Well-Being

Protecting family or loved ones shows important bonds in the characters' lives, lets us know their priorities, and can showcase selflessness – all admirable qualities in a character. In the film *1917*, two soldiers must race across enemy lines to stop an attack by 1600 of their fellow soldiers, that will see massive casualties. Certainly, their own lives are at stake, but it is the cost of so many others' lives that drives the emotional stakes of the storyline.

This stake can help to redeem a character who might otherwise come across as greedy or selfish. Goals can be short-term, near-sighted endeavors for a character. But if the longer-term consequences that are motivating them are more generous, then the stakes are useful for bringing out the manganous, altruistic qualities of a character.

Social or Familial Order

This is similar to the risk for others' well-being but addresses a more specific circumstance when a way of life is being protected from outside forces. For instance, in *The Godfather*, Michael Corleone takes the reins of the family to protect his ailing father, but what is really at stake – in a deeper and more substantive way – is whether the Corleone family and its traditional rules and mores that govern its power and wealth will be able to survive the threats from the rival mob families of New York as well as the changing times.

The John Milius film *Red Dawn* puts America's fate at stake under the threat of a Russian attack. Yes, others' well-being is at stake, and the lives of the protagonists (a group of well-armed high school students) are at stake, but by putting an entire democracy at stake, Milius can make a film that is larger in scope and bigger in theme than the specific actions in the film might make it seem.

Property

One of the most common stakes in movies is property, which can mean any number of things from money to treasure to jewelry. In the John Huston film *The Maltese Falcon*, the struggle between the central characters is for a jeweled falcon statue. In the Stanley Kubrick film *The Killing*, a pile of cash is at stake as the criminal characters vie for the upper hand. The property itself doesn't even need to take a specific form, as the notion of a MacGuffin – where the sought-after property is never named, like the contents of a briefcase in *Pulp Fiction* – and, dramatically, it is enough to know that this property is important to a character about whom we care for the audience to feel its importance as well.

It is worth noting that in this description, the property can feel like either a goal, what's at stake, or both. That is, money is the goal in *The Killing*, but it is also a stake in that the characters will lose that thing if they fail. Indeed, part of what works well about the GoFaSt model is that this flexibility – where goals and stakes can be interchangeable – is valuable. What's more important is the order of things – we start with the goal, and then get to the stakes. But whether a particular *thing* in a movie is a goal or a stake, it can simply be either, depending on how the film treats the thing itself.

Destiny

This stake usually pertains to the importance of achievement or the realization of one's purpose in life. This can be an athlete finding victory, such as in the running film *Chariots of Fire*, or an athlete finding if not victory, then redemption, such as Rocky Balboa losing in the climactic fight to Apollo Creed in *Rocky*. In this fight loss, he nevertheless wins the respect that he was seeking. Often, when a character's destiny is at stake, this could be them finding their true and authentic selves, such as the character Elbe transitioning to a woman at the end of *The Danish Girl*. What is at stake is one's value as a human or one's truth.

In Carl Theodore Dreyer's film *The Passion of Joan of Arc*, there are several things at stake. Joan's life is certainly at stake, given that she is on trial for a crime that will see her executed, but even more important than her life is her fealty to God. Her destiny is to sacrifice her life for God, and if she caves under the stress of torture and humiliation in the trial, then she risks losing her destiny.

In *Taxi Driver*, Travis Bickle is defending his own life as well as the life of a young woman forced into prostitution, but in the film's climactic scenes, what is also at stake is Travis's destiny – or, at least, his perceived destiny – as a hero, a savior who belongs in the headlines of newspapers. His own life is fairly meaningless to him; we come to believe about this character, but realizing his own mythology becomes the more important struggle.

Conclusion

"Give them the same, but different." This is an adage of Hollywood writing meant to illuminate two important, but seemingly contradictory, desires that audiences have for a film or episodic show. An experience that is too new or too dissimilar from anything they have previously seen can alienate or confuse an audience. A movie like this – that strikes its own path – can be viewed as *avant garde*, but quite often, it won't be viewed very much at

44 Stakes

all. Audiences usually prefer to have some pretext for a film or show that is familiar to them or at least has set some basic expectations for what they are about to experience. This is one of the enduring appeals of the genre: audiences generally know what they're in for. At the same time, if the film or show is *too* familiar with other films, then the audience will likely reject that film too, for being predictable or a "rip off." Hence: same thing but different – the sweet spot between pleasantly familiar and innovative.

This concept is valuable at the macro-level, from one movie to the next, and valuable at the micro-level, when comparing one GoFaSt cycle to the next within a single film. Each cycle should be the same thing (in as much as they should all feel part of the same broader story), but different (so they are not repetitive).

The shift in stakes, from one cycle to the next, is the tool that allows the *difference* to occur. While the change in goal from one cycle to the next is important to giving shape and momentum to the larger narrative, it is the change in stakes that provides a sense of difference in the feel, tone, and intensity of the story.

Study Guide

This chapter examines the concept of stakes and how they relate to establishing the theme of the movie. By putting at risk something of value to the protagonist – such as their safety, their pride, the well-being of others, etc. – the audience gets to learn about the worldview of the protagonist. As the stakes change from one cycle to the next, the audience gets to see the protagonist changing as a character, or – if not exactly changing – then the audience is able to learn about different aspects of who the character is.

As with the previous two chapters' study guides, go ahead and diagram the story of a chosen movie, or your own screenplay, and make note of the things that are at stake in the movie. What is at stake for the protagonist, or for other characters, during the course of the movie? If there is just one thing at stake during the entire script (such as the protagonist's own life if they are trying to escape a perilous situation), regardless of the intensity of the action or creativity of your protagonist's escapes and attacks, only having one thing at stake may lead the script feeling flat. Look for ways to use the failures in the script as a way to tackle a new idea or to put something else at stake. Perhaps the movie begins with your character's life at stake, and the story eventually puts their legacy, the lives of others, or patriotic duty at stake. Expand your own ideas about what your movie is truly about. What are you saying about the world where these characters live, whether it is a world of hope or one of decline? What can save this world, or what elements might doom it?

If exploring unexpected and interesting failures for your protagonist is an exercise in getting to know who they are and making them richer and deeper as people, putting things at stake is a way to step back from your script and think more broadly about the world in which these characters live. Take note of how "big" the stakes are in the movie you are analyzing or the script you are writing. Stakes are an important tool for modulating the scope of a story, and adjusting the scope is an important way to continually re-engage the audience as the movie plays out. For instance, saving one's life is important, but saving a community is more so, and saving an entire nation or social cause – potentially – is even greater. Do your stakes increase in scope through the course of the movie? Alternatively, the stakes can become smaller but more intimate, and therefore more meaningful, as the movie progresses. The stakes do not need to grow, as a rule, but they should change and continue to be meaningful.

References

Anderson, Paul Thomas (2007) *There Will Be Blood*. Paramount.
Avildsen, John G. (1976) *Rocky*. United Artists.
DeSica, Vittorio (1948) *Bicycle Thieves*. Ente Nazionale Industrie.
Dreyer, Carl Theodore (1928) *The Passion of Joan of Arc*. Societe Generale des Films.
Hooper, Tom (2015) *The Danish Girl*. Focus Features.
Hudson, Hugh (1981) *Chariots of Fire*. 20th Century Fox.
Huston, John (1941) *The Maltese Falcon*. Warner Bros.
Kiarostami, Abbas (1987) *Where is the Friend's House?* Kanoon.
Kubrick, Stanley (1956) *The Killing*. United Artists.
Lumet, Sidney (1975) *Dog Day Afternoon*. Warner Bros.
Mendes, Sam (2019) *1917*. Universal Pictures.
Milius, John (1984) *Red Dawn*. United Artists.
Reichardt, Kelly (2008) *Wendy and Lucy*. Oscilloscope Pictures.
Safdie, Josh and Benny (2019) *Uncut Gems*. A24.
Scorsese, Martin (1976) *Taxi Driver*. Columbia Pictures.
Stanton, Andrew (2008) *Wall-E*. Walt Disney Pictures.
Tarantino, Quentin (1994) *Pulp Fiction*. Miramax Films.

The GoFaSt Guide to Screenwriting

5

GOFAST EXERCISE

Writing a Sample Horror Movie

Overview of the Horror Genre

Horror has been a steadfastly popular genre throughout the history of cinema and across the world. Films such as F. W. Murnau's silent film *Nosferatu* and the recent and extraordinary Ari Aster film *Midsommar* have delivered some of cinema's greatest offerings to the movie-going public. Sub-genres, such as slasher films and psychological horror films, have enriched the genre and shown that, in countless incarnations across time and nations, audiences love to be scared. Plenty of theories exist to explain why horror movies are of such importance to audiences. One frequently stated theory is that horror films can be cathartic. When viewed from the safety of one's seat, horror films allow the audience to experience their fears, confront them, and process them without being harmed. To safely confront one's fears can be a meaningful and even healing experience.

Another theory is that horror films entice an audience's curiosity about the mysteries of the world. In the same way that mythologies were conceived, in part, to explain the unknowns of the universe, horror offers its own explanations about what inexplicable things happen in a usually rational world. Maybe that bump upstairs was caused by ghosts. Or maybe *we're* the ghosts. Spells and curses, visitations by the undead and evil spirits, offer an alternative (and extremely entertaining) knowledge, or possible knowledge, about the secrets of the world. Humans, endlessly curious and imaginative and often prone to superstitions, are perfectly suited to relish in the strangeness and thrills of the horror genre.

The box office power behind horror demonstrates that this appeal is more than theoretical, and unlike superhero movies, which are usually more

DOI: 10.4324/9781003141549-5

expensive to produce and require giant box office returns, horror can sometimes be made on the cheap (as far as movies go, which is never truly cheap in an absolute sense) and still appeal to huge audiences. *The Blair Witch Project* and *The Babadook* are examples of low-to-modestly budgeted horror movies tapping the right nerve of fear in the audience and cashing in commercially.

The horror genre is remarkably flexible. The conventions of horror can remain open because the genre is not tied to any specific location, time period, or style of storytelling. What defines horror is its capacity to scare the audience, and therefore the genre can continue to be remade and feel new as tastes and trends change. The Western genre is generally more constrained by a certain setting (the western United States) and time period (late nineteenth century), and while there are certainly notable examples of Westerns that push into different times and places (Quentin Tarantino famously described *Django Unchained* as a "southern" – that is, a western film set in the American South), most westerns fit the genre mold in order to maintain the western moniker. This is perhaps one of the reasons that Westerns go in and out of style and sometimes struggle with feeling relevant to audiences.

All genres are capable of being blended with other genres, but horror's conventional openness allows it to be particularly adept at being made fresh and new with genre cross-pollination. From horror-sci-fi (the *Alien* franchise) to horror-westerns (*From Dusk Till Dawn*), to horror-superhero (*Hellboy*), to horror-comedy (*Shaun of the Dead*), horror remains perennially fresh and new – and is an intriguing starting point for this chapter's writing exercise.

Writing a New Film

These next three chapters show how the GoFaSt model can be used to outline screenplays in various genres. By starting with a basic premise within the horror genre, these next pages will use the cycles of establishing goals, failures, and stakes to map out the story of a script.

Let's start with a premise. For purposes here, let's work within the parameters of some recent horror films that operate in the low-to-moderate budget range. Some terrific films have emerged from this space, from *Hereditary* to *The Babadook*, which blend elements of psychological horror with jump-scare horror and stories crafted from family situations revolving around a tragedy. *Midsommar*, Ari Aster's follow-up film to *Hereditary*, involves a similar story and tonal qualities. In *Midsommar*, protagonist Dani begins the film terrified that her sister may have committed suicide. In reaching out to her boyfriend through a series of frantic messages, Dani discovers that the reality of her sister's fate is worse than Dani's most awful fears: her sister has not only committed suicide but killed their parents as well. It is a powerfully dramatic and horrific opening, setting the stage for the darkness of the events that are about to befall Dani and her friends on a subsequent trip to Sweden.

48 GoFaSt Exercise

For the sake of working within this intriguing recent space, let's come up with a premise about a family recovering from a recent, tragic event to give the story a firm foothold for the first cycle. These recent films also work within contained locations: the family home in *Hereditary* and *The Babadook*, and a small rural village in *Midsommar*. If our family is looking to get away from home to a quiet place to recover from the tragedy, we'd have to figure out where they are going. Keeping within a low or moderate budget, somewhere rural is going to be more affordable than a city or more populated destination. This could be a second home that they own, perhaps a home in the country. Alternatively, this could be a family of more modest means, so they're traveling to a place where they're renting a house. For the sake of argument, let's reverse *The Babadook* setup and have a mother who has died and a father taking care of his two children. The family is devastated by the accidental death of the mom, and they're heading out to a house somewhere quiet to heal.

Instinctively, you may feel some things about your story moving forward that you want to embrace or avoid. The intimacy of *The Babadook* is deeply compelling and fits with the notion of a family traveling somewhere to heal. With two children and two of the major characters, there could likely be some coming-of-age elements to the story. If coming-of-age is about leaving the comforts and protections that childhood is supposed to embody to learn about the harshness and unknowns of real life, then horror naturally creates fascinating options for what that harshness might look and feel like.

We have not yet delved into the GoFaSt cycles but have engaged in essentially a creative word-association type of exercise of taking some recent trends in the genre and developing a premise that feels both familiar to a story design that can work well while giving some fresh narrative elements. A few early, logical decisions, based on budget (low-to-moderate), tone (intimate relationship or family-based horror, as opposed to slasher-type horror), and adding in a subgenre to mix with the horror (coming-of-age), already put our story on solid ground to begin work.

Cycle One

Goals

Is this premise developed enough to go on to start writing the first cycle? We can preview the work of the first cycle – creating a goal for the protagonist – to test this question. If we're to think about the father in the story having to look after two children while mourning his wife's death, what might his goal be? The goal must be specific and actionable and relate to traveling to a second home so that the family might mourn and recover. What roadblocks might he encounter in achieving this goal? Failures will add complications to the story and allow new story elements to infiltrate the narrative. Perhaps there could be a problem with the house – recent flooding while the family was distracted by the funeral – or something that happens to the family on the trip to the house.

Neither of these ideas is necessarily bad, but they also don't – from an instinctive level – seem to offer much in the way of exceedingly interesting failures brewing on the narrative horizon. When this happens, consider adjusting the premise to put the protagonist in more difficult or awkward circumstances. A screenwriter's instinct should usually tend toward making the events of the story harder on the protagonist when things do not feel right in the script.

What could make this situation trickier for the protagonist (at this point, let's give him a name and call him Sean)? We could change the circumstances of the trip. Perhaps another family has invited Sean and his two children to this house. Sean's modest financial situation, especially after paying for the funeral, is interesting and makes his situation harder for him. So, another family, seeking to give Sean and his two children (we can name them as well, Violet and Henry) the distraction and peace that they need, has invited them for a getaway. The goal is the same: to go to a quiet place for a brief period of time, but now we have an invitation – both generous and potentially awkward – a house that is not Sean's and therefore unfamiliar, and another set of characters against whom Sean and his kids might clash.

Failures

Sean's goal is specific: to bring his children to a get-away home in the woods where the peace and quiet, and healing properties of nature might help them mourn the recent death of their mother. This goal is also ripe with the potential for failure. Let's say the house is not in great shape. Perhaps it's an utter disaster. The area is beautiful, but the pictures online that advertised the house are quite old, and the house is in extreme disrepair. Perhaps the picture online is an old photo and not representative of its current state; additionally, if this is a new listing on the rental website, then no reviews exist to indicate the problem with the house. Regardless, Sean did not choose it himself, and the state of the house, therefore, doesn't require much more explanation than what we already have.

A second realm of failure could relate to an interpersonal failure between the families. There must be some friendliness between the families for the invitation to have occurred (unless the invitation is a trap of some sort), or perhaps the families do not know each other well and their only connection is the deceased mother. They all knew her – but Sean does not know this family very well.

Let's use the first failure to connect this story with the coming-of-age subplot. Violet, Sean's older child, may have a rivalry – or is getting bullied –

with the other family's eldest daughter of the same age, Tara. There may be a grudge between the two girls that Sean was not aware of, and Violet is threatened by Tara in some way. What is at the heart of this conflict, and does this need to be figured out now? It may not be necessary to understand the backstory yet.

What is important here – for using the model to outline the story – is that we have a goal and a failure. The goal is for Sean and the children seeking refuge at a nature getaway to recover from the shock of their mother's death, and the failure is that the refuge is not much of a refuge, and the solace that they were seeking is interrupted by the appearance of Tara, who has put Violet in some sort of jeopardy. Enough story information is in place to allow us to keep moving forward with writing the cycle; although if a roadblock emerges ahead, it is always possible to return to this blank space and fill it in with a subplot that could motivate a later storyline.

Stakes

What is at stake with these failures? The story begins with Sean and his children dealing with grief and loss. The disrepair of the house means that now their safety might be at risk, and for Violet personally, she is threatened by a rude girl who seeks to bother and bully her.

These stakes are not as big as the grief for their mother (unless the safety in the house is a significant and immediate threat), but as discussed earlier, stakes do not need to grow in scope. They do not need to get "bigger." This conventional wisdom is rather limiting and closes off options for where a writer might want to take their story. What is more important is the change in stakes that gives the story a natural feeling of progression and evolution. What is most important, when it comes to stakes is that they matter to the character – a character who is shifting, changing, and growing during the movie. And as people change, so do the stakes in their lives – sometimes bigger, sometimes smaller – but it's the change that's important that at each moment of change, they might lose something of value, until the end of the movie, when that character has arrived at a more complete version of themselves or comes up short and tragically loses.

Cycle Two

Goals

The second cycle begins with a new goal. The previous cycle saw failures in the house that was supposed to give them respite (it's old, creepy, and possibly dangerous) and in the family whose generosity was meant to comfort the grieving survivors (Violet is bullied by another girl). What are some possible responses to this? If the situation is dire enough, Sean could load his kids into the car and make an awkward exit from the weekend. This goal might lead nowhere in terms of the plot because they're likely just going back home, and the story will have wasted its first cycle.

But if the situation is merely bothersome, or only slightly concerning, then horrible, then a more moderated goal could continue the premise moving forward without having to abandon it. The first cycle's failure, then, should not be too extreme to allow Sean and the kids to be willing to continue to give this weekend a try. Failures are not meant to stop the protagonist in their journey; rather, failures will challenge their resilience and press them to try a new tactic to get the thing they need. In the process of challenging them, the audience gets to know them, and the story can move to a new setting or direction.

As a response to the failure, Sean could suggest temporarily leaving the house to clear the tension and have a clear head before deciding what to do about the house. Perhaps there's a street fair going on in town, and the two families also want to stop by a store to buy groceries for a barbecue. Perhaps a good meal and some entertainment will help give a lighter perspective to the events that have so far occurred. Also, being out together, maybe Sean will have a chance to check in with the other parents about their daughter's behavior.

The first cycle has established, Sean as a caring father who is willing to do anything, and go anywhere, to help his kids through this tough time. We also see that, by going away on the weekend, he is perhaps overwhelmed by grief himself and therefore unable to manage the kids' struggles on his own. So, he is caring and thoughtful, but also nearing his emotional limits. By going into town as a response to a difficult entry to the weekend, Sean also shows himself to be patient and level-headed – the type of person who is useful in a crisis.

We have solid amounts of plot and character development, but for a horror movie, no scares yet. The mother's death could certainly be a scary scene, and the location of a decrepit house that's sort of rotting from the inside is also creepy, and perhaps the bullying daughter is strange and unsettling, but so far, the horror in this movie is a slow burn. This is not necessarily a bad thing, as many horror movies take some time to set up the story before diving into the thrills – it's just important to understand, as the screenwriter, where the script is in terms of the expectations of the genre. All of this to say, the second cycle is the time to ramp up the creepiness factor.

Therefore, let's build the town. Perhaps this is a village in the mountains, a very remote location. The isolation is a trope for this type of story, but it's also useful: it works to ramp up the fear. Being cut off from civilization is well-suited for this story because it suggests the de-stressing that the family seeks while also increasing the risk of being alone in case something goes wrong. The town should be frightful; something is off about everyone. The threat should be more psychological. Film history provides intriguing models of terrifying towns for a protagonist to navigate their way through, from the villa in Carl Theodore Dreyer's *Vampyr*, where locals are seen engaging in odd activities, and shadows are seen digging ditches and dancing around while unattached to people, to Robert Weine's *The Cabinet of Dr. Caligari*, where residents in town seem to move about as if under a hypnotic spell. One film that took this notion of a somnambulist population of villagers to a literal level is Werner Herzog's *Heart of Glass*, where the entire cast was hypnotized prior to filming their scenes. The result is an unnerving ensemble of performances from the locals, as they move and speak their lines in a dazed, inhuman manner.

One can imagine the town that our protagonists enter to be similarly strange, where the locals are perhaps bizarrely distant and odd. This would make Sean's goal hard to achieve – which is one of the requirements of a goal in the GoFaSt model. If the two families came to town hoping for some shopping and experiences that might lift their moods, running into this strange place would certainly make that goal hard to achieve. Instead of finding local charm, they find locals like the ones in *Heart of Glass*. Given that this is a forested location, perhaps there is a local drug, some sort of fungi naturally grown, that is widespread in town and the basis of many of the local rituals and activities. The two families, hoping to walk into town for nothing more than finding a fresh bakery and some regional arts and crafts, find a town of people strangely zombified by a mysterious, homegrown drug.

Failures

This experience leads to the failure of the second cycle's goal. The two families return home with minor successes (groceries have been purchased, let's say, for a dinner barbecue), but they feel paranoid and threatened by what they saw. One of the structural uses of failure is that it tells us something about an individual's character. Each character who fails in a certain manner will reveal aspects of their personalities and histories that are relevant to the screenwriter's ability to have the audience truly know who these characters are. So, although they suffer a collective failure as a group, let's assign some individuals' failures as well.

Perhaps the two fathers, Sean and Paul, go off together in town for some bonding and conversation. How could this effort prove a failure for Sean? If Sean went along with Paul for support, this support gets nullified. Perhaps Paul is swayed by the local experimentations and indulges in their use of these strange local fungi, and Sean is either threatened or finds himself dosed by these fungi as well. Meanwhile, Violet faces a different kind of continuing failure in town that proves to further isolate them. Perhaps this means a run-in with local law enforcement, such as a sheriff, shows that the two families are under threat, and they are not safe in this town at all.

Stakes

A return to the house that evening showed an increase in stakes. Sean has a bad trip, perhaps encouraged by Paul, which brings back the trauma of Sean's wife's death. And Violet is now aware that the local sheriff has a vendetta against the family. This could relate to the house that either has not been rented in a long time or this is the first rental. Perhaps the house was mistakenly rented, and when the two families showed up, their presence was seen as a threat to the locals.

Any of these plot directions could be expanded, but importantly for the purposes of this model, they all stem from the shared need to show a goal, failure, and an increase in stakes. If Violet was threatened by the bullying behavior of the other family's daughter, now she sees that the whole town now has a grudge against them. Sean, occupied by a bad trip that has left him struggling to manage his own mental health and grief, worries about his sanity and ability to continue to provide care for his two children.

Cycle Three

Goals

Goals can be used to explore different facets of the story and allow the screenwriter the freedom and mobility to shift around the plot if things begin feeling repetitive. Traditional models can tend to make the screenwriter feel beholden to following a single trajectory in the script. As an example of how looking at screenwriting through the lens of the GoFaSt model provides flexibility in the outline, the later chapter that analyzes *There Will Be Blood* makes a case for how each cycle can shift focus on different characters while maintaining cohesion in the script.

If the first two cycles have focused on Sean and Violet, this cycle can bring another character into focus: Sean's youngest child, whom we could call Henry. In the aftermath of Sean's bad trip and Violet's struggle, Henry has his own issue.

Let's say he is lured by another local kid and brought into the woods. The kid reveals some backstory about the town secrets that have to do with exotic fungi being grown in the area, and the whole town is consumed by these mushrooms. It's an almost symbiotic relationship between people and this strange fungus. Henry learns that the locals are using the families at the rental house as a sort of experiment because a certain spore has been found in the house. The locals want to see what happens to them. Henry is now missing in the woods, taken hostage by this strange and threatening kid, and Henry's goal is to escape back to the house so that he can tell his family the news.

Failures

If Henry has been kidnapped in the woods, but we want Sean to ultimately succeed in his larger goal of providing security to his children, then Sean can find Henry, but the efforts of finding him come at a great cost. This is an intriguing version of failure in the model because it allows a character the strength and wherewithal to succeed at a goal while applying great drama and hardship that proves their mettle. Let's say that the strange boy's assertions about this experimental fungus afflicting the families in the house are shown to be true, and while Henry is being kidnapped, the families are being overcome with terrible sickness or terror at the fungi's effects. Sean must fight through these effects (which could include terrible hallucinations or sensory deprivation issues such as temporary blindness) to try to find Henry.

Sean eventually locates Henry, but the failure is that Sean has endured terrible suffering, and everyone back at the house is enduring this suffering as well. The fungus is making them all sick and terrified, while the sheriff and locals are perhaps descending on the house to observe this science experiment, of sorts, that they use the rental house to lure these two families to endure.

Stakes

The stakes are higher now, as the fungus has put everyone's lives in danger inside the house. They are sick and hallucinating, and whereas in earlier cycles their mental well-being was at stake, the much larger and more critical issue of survival is now at stake. The characters are in the position of having to fight for their lives. Additionally, the story implies that these two families would not be the only victims of these villains. Other characters, in the future, may find themselves as unwitting specimens of the experiments and exploits of these dangerous locals. For our protagonists to survive and defeat the villains, means, more lives might also be saved.

Cycle Four

Goals

In this final cycle, the goal is inevitable: the families must escape the house. If the two families were at odds with each other, this ending would either see Sean and his kids proving victorious in these confrontations or the two families learning to come to terms with each other, depending on how the screenwriter would want to play the final scenes. The former is somewhat more of a savage ending, and the latter potentially provides more hope.

Regardless, they must escape the house and the town. Doing so would also probably see a final confrontation with the sheriff and whatever locals were seen as particularly prevalent antagonists in the story.

Failures

The screenwriter has a choice about whether to, indeed, make this final cycle end in failure or not. Or perhaps have an ending that is in between the two outcomes. A failure would see the families perhaps killed in their efforts, and like a spider web set for the next victims, the house put back on the rental market for the next unsuspecting guests to be experimented on. This is certainly a dark, though interesting, ending.

But as the model suggests, the failure part of the final cycle can also be a success, and we see Sean prove to be the parent he had been seeking to be from the beginning – someone who can protect his kids – and he manages to save them while defeating the antagonists and, perhaps, destroying the house so that no more ills can come to anyone else.

Stakes

The final cycle also sees the stakes part of the cycle operate somewhat differently, given that with the story ending, nothing really is at stake for characters whom the audience will no longer see. Therefore, this section is used as a thematic summation of the story. What larger question had been asked about these characters or the world? The theme of protection seems to be an important one, and the possibility of healing that exists in a world that is dangerous, unpredictable, and sometimes – as the events this story have shown – downright evil.

Conclusion

This sample movie does not feature ghosts or paranormal activity, but in many ways, it operates like a haunted house horror story. Part of the fun of the horror genre is its flexibility in mixing and matching conventional tropes with new ideas. The goals of the characters, in this exercise, resemble the types of goals one would expect if the house was besieged by ghosts instead of fungus. By changing the nature of the threat, the tried-and-true conventions of a haunted house movie can feel fresh. Goals are about plot and structure, and haunted house stories – while they may seem predictable and old-fashioned at first consideration – can be perennially interesting if the failures that the protagonists encounter are new and unconventional.

Earlier in this book, the notion of "the same thing, but different" was discussed. That is, many audiences want new stories that feel fresh and unexpected and address the current social landscape, but they don't want their movies to feel entirely dissimilar from the ones they already love. Many conventional templates and genres remain commercially appealing and creatively sound. Movies and stories do not need to be entirely re-invented just to feel contemporary. By breaking down conventional stories or genres into cycles of goals, failures, and stakes, it is possible to freshen up old standards and genres by replacing the types of failures that the characters usually experience.

References

Anderson, Paul Thomas (2007) *There Will Be Blood*. Paramount.
Aster, Ari (2018) *Hereditary*. A24.
Aster, Ari (2019) *Midsommar*. A24.
Dreyer, Carl Theodore (1932) *Vampyr*. Vereinigte Star-Film.
Herzog, Werner (1976) *Heart of Glass*. Werner Herzog Filmproduktion.
Kent, Jennifer (2014) *The Babadook*. Umbrella Entertainment.
Marshall, Neil (2019) *Hellboy*. Lionsgate.
Myrick, Daniel and Sanchez, Eduardo (1999) *The Blair Witch Project*. Artisan Entertainment.
Rodriguez, Robert (1996) *From Dusk Till Dawn*. Miramax Films.
Tarantino, Quentin (2012) *Django Unchained*. The Weinstein Company.
Weine, Robert (1920) *The Cabinet of Dr. Caligari*.
Wright, Edgar (2004) *Shaun of the Dead*. Universal Pictures.

The GoFaSt Guide to Screenwriting

6

GOFAST EXERCISE

Writing a Sample Superhero Movie

The superhero genre is generally loved by audiences, occasionally appreciated by critics, and famously scorned by various filmmakers. Regardless of one's opinion about the cinematic worthiness of superhero movies, their collective cultural footprint is undeniable. These are – usually – the movies that demand the largest production and marketing budgets in Hollywood, and except for an occasional miss with audiences, they are an extremely reliable financial bet for producers and studios.

The popularity of this genre has been steadfast and growing for years, and Hollywood's ability to export these films to worldwide audiences is enormously successful. Indeed, their very existence is predicated upon reaching the widest possible audiences around the world – and appealing to an audience's sense of awe, romance, laughter, and compassion for these suffering and heroic supernatural or technologically gifted characters. These emotional responses are familiar to what audiences sought in Hollywood's earliest films, from Chaplin's movies (full of laughter and romance) to Buster Keaton's movies (full of laughter and awe at the physical stunts) to early commercial successes like the 1927 film *Seventh Heaven* that achieved all these reactions from audiences.

Perhaps part of the success of the superhero genre is that, while the films themselves represent enormous technical achievements from when the Hollywood studio system began over a century ago, many of the cinematic principles that worked from the beginning are still working today.

DOI: 10.4324/9781003141549-6

Cycle One

Goals

Given the cultural relevance and popularity of the superhero genre, let's construct a superhero film using the GoFaSt model – to see an example of how the model can be employed. Starting this process without a specific sense of plot direction or characters, we'll walk through how to build the structure for a script from the "ground up."

We can begin the structuring with some basic assumptions about the genre itself. Superhero films are usually about a superhero having to protect or save something. In our scenario, we can open with this question: what is the superhero trying to save? A town? A city? A person or a group of people? The whole world?

For the sake of creating an opportunity for the story to build, let's start small and say with *a person*. Given restrictions on intellectual property that are closely guarded by the studios, we'll have to make up our own superhero. Because we're starting from zero, as it were, as opposed to building from a franchise, starting small in scope makes sense – it will give us ample room and time to introduce this new superhero.

Taking logical steps to continue to build the story – and understanding that we must begin the cycle with a goal for the superhero – two clear questions emerge:

1) What is endangering this person?
2) Why is the superhero trying to save this person (beyond generic altruism)?

There are many worthwhile directions to go in answering these questions. This person who needs saving – let's call her Emily – could have secret information that evil forces are trying to obtain. Or she could have a superpower, herself, that makes her valuable to others. Both explanations are familiar to the genre but, from a story perspective, certainly viable.

However, given that some superhero movies have recently developed a more gritty, realistic tone (such as *Joker* and *Birds of Prey*), let's go with something less extreme and more human: a jealous lover is threatening Emily. Emily is trying to leave this lover (we can call him Mark), and Mark is refusing to let her go. Our superhero must step in. We're beginning to figure out the superhero's goal.

Now, admittedly, this plotting does not feel terribly "superhero"-like, but again, referencing *Joker*, where real-life scenarios such as mental illness and loneliness are motivating superheroes (and these motivations are treated as dramas more than the fanciful, archetypal stories that they used to be), this set-up could work. We can move forward with a classic unrequited love triangle situation where Emily is trying to leave Mark, and the superhero – in trying to save her – is, at some level, in love with her too.

As we know from the chapter on goals, it is important that the goal should be both actionable and hard to achieve. It is clearly actionable: the superhero is trying to get Emily away from Mark. But to "get her away" does not feel verifiable. How far away does the superhero need to get her? Does "get away" mean that the superhero wants to ensure that Mark does not see her again? Or talk to her again? And what would prevent Mark from seeing or talking to her from one day to the next? We need to drill down and better crystalize the goal to fulfill the qualities that are laid out in Chapter 2.

What goal can convey a sense of finality? The superhero could be trying to move out of town with Emily, or he could try to kill Mark. This second idea feels somewhat intense to start off the movie. That isn't necessarily a bad thing, but for our purposes in this exercise, let's continue the philosophy of starting smaller in scope and slower in pace.

If Mark and Emily are living together, then her moving out of the house is very specific. This is an actionable, verifiable, and straightforward goal. Could Mark follow her and later confront her? Yes. However, the goal does not need to solve all her problems – it just needs to be something that has a clear finish line that the audience can see has either worked or not worked.

If the superhero's goal is to help get her – and her belongings – out of the house, how do we make this goal hard? We could make Mark a physical threat to Emily (perhaps she is leaving him because he is abusive), and the superhero's goal is to make sure that they get her out of the house safely.

We have not established what type of powers this superhero has. Generally, superheroes are either mutants or aliens (and their powers are inherent within them), or they are regular people and their powers have been acquired by the use of a suit or special object. Either way, one would assume that whatever powers our superhero possesses, and however they may have been ordained upon him, any powers would give the protagonist a significant advantage in dispatching with a regular human like Mark. Imagine Spiderman or Superman needing to dispatch with an ordinary person – it wouldn't be a fair fight.

So how do we make this goal hard for the superhero? There are many options. Perhaps the superhero must keep his powers secret (like Superman or Spiderman), and he's unable to use them publicly (i.e., in front of Mark). Alternatively, Mark might also have superpowers. This would make our protagonist's goal harder, but pitting two characters with superpowers head-to-head at the start of the movie might be a bit overloaded when we don't yet know who any of these characters are. So let's consider the idea that the superhero must achieve this specific goal of safely ensuring that Emily can move out of the house (the goal is verifiable), and the superhero must hide his powers while doing so (the goal is difficult).

By adhering to the principles of GoFaSt, the writer is in a position of working the story in a productive way rather than merely accumulating pages without intention. The plot and character intentions are clearer because following the model creates specific questions that the writer must answer. The superhero must keep his powers secret, which raises the question of why? What does it say about the character that he must be so cautious?

Perhaps his powers hurt someone accidentally, and he is reluctant to use them again. This idea might give us an opening scene to the movie that initiates the tone of the genre: we see his powers going awry and an innocent person (perhaps related to Emily) getting hurt or killed. This backstory could provide some layers and depth to the superhero and Emily's relationship, depending on how it's played. For instance, if Emily knows that the superhero is responsible, or does not know, would open different types of doors for where the story would go. Those questions don't need to be answered now, though, because the model has put this structural point into place and given the script a solid foundation. Later in the writing process, the writer can explore which avenue to take.

Going further with this idea, perhaps the superhero is trying to get rid of his powers because he doesn't want to hurt anyone else in the future. There could be an interesting concept that he's trying to figure out a way to somehow drain his superpowers out of his body, and Emily – or Mark – has a unique ability (whether they realize it or not) to help the superhero achieve this.

Certainly, much of the backstory and details of this set-up remain to be figured out, but by adhering to the principles of this first stage of the GoFaSt cycle, we're productively putting together major elements of the story, compiling useful information about the characters, and instigating the plot.

Failures

The second phase of the cycle will feature the superhero failing. The superhero wants to get Emily safely out of Mark's house – whether this be via stealth in the middle of the night or in full view of Mark – and in some way, the superhero must fail.

One obvious idea is, perhaps Mark kills Emily during the escape. The superhero will have certainly failed, and this event could set us up for writing an interesting revenge-superhero movie. But let's say that we want to keep Emily in the story for the sake of developing a romance. In that case, how else could he fail? Perhaps there's a fight between Mark and the superhero, and Emily fears that the superhero has been killed. With the fatal fight as a distraction to Mark, now Emily can escape on her own. The superhero, recovering from the encounter, must find her. He has failed at his initial task (safely getting her out of the house) because even though she is indeed out, she's still in danger. Depending on where she's gone, she might be in even more danger now. Mark, as we can establish at this point, is an antagonist with dangerous connections. Perhaps he's a mobster or a member of a nefarious secret organization, and this gives him the resources to find Emily.

Failures, as we know, should complicate the story – open it up to new plotlines and characters. When writing a failure, we don't need to know what all the plotlines might be – rather, we just need to pursue the direction that feels like it might give us the most options – or open the most doors for how the next cycle might play out.

For instance, by having Emily escape, at least two plotlines ensue: the superhero must find her, and Mark will also be hunting her down.

Additionally, this failure has also put the writer in a strong position of having a visual sequence: it necessitates that Mark and the superhero will fight, the confrontation will be extremely dangerous, and Emily will find a way – in the middle of the commotion – to flee.

Stakes

The third phase of the cycle is "stakes." How have the stakes changed during this cycle? Emily began the cycle in danger of Mark (that's why she was trying to leave), but now she has wronged him more acutely (though heroically) and his anger toward her will be more intense. Additionally, the superhero is now in danger from Mark, given their confrontation. And whereas Emily was previously in danger from Mark, the superhero was at least nearby to help give her some sense of security. Now she is on her own. The stakes have increased for both of our sympathetic characters. As the second cycle begins, they are in a more precarious position than when the first cycle started.

Stakes can be a place for the themes of the story to emerge. We don't yet have a definitive theme appearing, but there is a sense of some larger ideas floating around the text: the idea of how much can people really save each other and how being untrue to oneself (think about the superhero hiding his powers) weakens them. The superhero will have to find some inner truth to save himself and Emily and to answer the question of whether we're fundamentally alone in the world or whether help is out there, somewhere, for us.

Cycle Two

Goals

The length of each GoFaSt cycle is usually about twenty to thirty-five pages. This doesn't have to be the case, however, since what is most important is the integrity of the cycle rather than page count. Nevertheless, looking at the amount of story we have come up with so far, we're likely in this page count range.

We're now starting the second cycle of the model. Once again, we begin with a goal. The most readily apparent goal for the superhero – given where the first cycle left off – is to find Emily. This goal is straightforward and verifiable: either he will find her, or he won't. Now let's think about what can make this goal hard to accomplish. The obstacles can lie with her (perhaps she doesn't want to be found, or she is in a location that will bring complexity to his search), or the obstacles can lie with the superhero (there is something about the location, or the nature of the search, that plays into his weaknesses rather than his strengths). The obstacles can also originate from both, and the writer can figure out ways to tie them together.

Let's start with Emily and her location – and then figure out how this location might be significant to the superhero.

This being a superhero movie, it makes sense to set her disappearance in a place that plays visually. An enormous city could work well. If there is a sci-fi element to the story, then maybe she escaped to a parallel dimension or outer space. Nothing we have come up with so far in the story suggests science fiction, but part of the appeal of GoFaSt is that it allows for brainstorming at each phase, and if an idea feels particularly compelling, then details can be added to the earlier cycles. For instance, if we *did* want to go this parallel dimension route, then we could add into the backstory scientific research that either Emily or Mark had done in hidden dimensions. Perhaps they are genius scientists, and the reason she is trying to leave him is not that he's abusive but that he's stealing her research. Or he intends to use her research for nefarious purposes. None of these additions change the structure of the story; the structure is sound, and the flexibility of the model allows for these adjustments to be made.

But for now, let's keep thinking about alternative locations. We could think of the opposite of the city and go for the desert – in the style of the Wolverine superhero movie *Logan*. Or we could consider an equally desolate location, like a forest.

Checking back on the requirements of the model, if we want to choose a forest, how would this location make the superhero's search hard? Well, forests tend to be large and difficult to traverse. It is easy to get lost. Starvation, thirst, and dangerous animals are clear risks. But if this is not a pure survivalism story, would these obstacles really be enough to make his goal hard? Possibly not. So let's figure out how to personalize the forest obstacles.

If we had considered the idea that somehow the superhero was trying to drain away his own powers, then the forest should do the opposite: it will increase his powers. Even without us specifically knowing what his powers are, this could be a compelling direction to explore. After all, the goal should play not toward a character's strengths but toward their weaknesses. If he fears his powers, then he'll have to deal with his powers in a very profound way in the forest.

What power could be dangerous? Traditional powers like invisibility or flight, or underwater breathing do not seem to be dangerous to the superhero wielding them. Something explosive would be dangerous – a power that could easily create lots of collateral damage. If the superhero's power was to create explosions – perhaps by touching his fists together – then we now have a few plot elements coming together that could make his goal hard.

The superhero's power is quite strong, but he doesn't want to use it for fear of hurting others. Whatever is lurking in the forest is making his powers more intense. The further he advances in the forest, he increasingly *has* to use his power. Like an errant boiler that needs a release of steam or risks blowing up, the superhero must regularly use his power – discharge it – to keep control of himself. Maybe he gets sick if the power builds up inside of him, or he becomes physically very heavy and exhausted carrying the accumulating power.

Without us having to figure out the details (again, this is just the structure we're putting together), this forest (or something in it) might be the origin of his powers. As if getting deeper into the forest makes his powers stronger, more volatile, and requiring more discharges to maintain his health.

Superheroes often have sidekicks. Our movie is meant to employ gritty realism, so a sidekick could be more of a friend – the one person who knows about his power. Perhaps this friend is a demolition expert. As the two search the forest looking for Emily, the superhero must occasionally unleash his power, and the friend could keep himself safe each time by using protective equipment that he carries with him.

If Mark is following them – also in search of Emily – then perhaps Mark sees one of these unleashes of power and becomes aware that the superhero has an enormous (and valuable) secret.

We now have a goal that is hard – both generically speaking, and specific to the superhero – and our attempts to uncover *why* it's hard have, in part, further developed the characters and this world.

Failures

The superhero might fail by being unable to find Emily. The most obvious idea is not necessarily a bad thing. Whether or not a plot element works often comes down to execution, and the writer should be wary of overcomplicating the plot just for the sake of not wanting to make the most clear-sighted choice. The superhero not finding Emily is perfectly fine as a failure, but we have some work to do. The issue is that *not* finding someone is not verifiable. The act of *not finding someone* can go on for days, weeks, or longer. There is nothing to declare that the search is over. Some exceptions are when the person being searched for is dead. A writer could take that route. Emily's death could lead the story in numerous directions – perhaps the superhero falls into depression and the story takes an internal direction, or the death is murder (Mark found her first and killed her) and the movie becomes a revenge story.

By following the model, options will open, and the screenwriter – like considering chess moves – can look ahead into the plot searching for the most fertile directions. Where would the story lead, given that there must be a subsequent increase in stakes and a new cycle with a new goal? Without a structural model, wondering "what happens next?" might lead the screenwriter into endlessly digressive paths that can take away from the core concept of the script. Instead, by thinking about how to satisfy the GoFaSt model with this question – what's the most interesting way for them to fail? – the script can remain on track while the screenwriter is given room to be creative.

Another way to make the failed search verifiable is to have the trail end *without* having found Emily. How do we indicate that the trail has ended? There must be a destination; perhaps the superhero has arrived at a town deep in the woods – a functioning town in the middle of nowhere. Perhaps this place appears to be an ordinary town (except for its unusual location), but in fact, it is a stronghold. A modern-day fort.

Why and how did Emily wind up here? Let's look at some of the facts of the story that the model has helped us develop. One thing we know about Mark is that he has dangerous and deep-running connections. We know this because Emily's escape in the first cycle must be hard, and Mark being a mobster, or being affiliated with a secret society, makes her escape a difficult endeavor.

Emily arrives at this town, which is probably related to Mark's connections. We can take this further and say that Mark's relatives, or perhaps his brothers, run this town. Emily knows that, and so she has come into the woods not just to escape but also to bring down the brothers and destroy Mark's influence. We don't know the nature of that influence yet, but structurally, we can use this as a placeholder to satisfy the directive we've been working toward: make the superhero's failure verifiable.

Failures are, as we know, flexible structural mechanisms. He has failed to find her at the end of the forest search, and the failure is now going to lead the story into the third cycle. But before getting to the third cycle, let's examine where we are with the final phase of this second cycle.

Stakes

The stakes in the first cycle drew a fine point to the danger that Emily is in. Now, we must see that she is in even more danger (by having arrived in the lion's den of her ex-lover's influence). We also see that – as the superhero has arrived – he is in heightened danger as well. Whatever the origin of his superpower, it probably comes from this place. Again, we don't yet have details on how that might be the case, but simply by following the model, we know that in some way, the potential consequences against our protagonist have increased. He has arrived at the stronghold, where not only Emily has arrived but where he must now contend with his own origin story.

By seeing these plot elements come together, it also seems likely that Mark has some earlier relationship to either the superhero or the superhero's powers. We don't yet know if Mark invented these powers, or he bequeathed them to the superhero (perhaps unknowingly), but the model is leading these plot elements together in a way that they're all pointing toward this town as significant – in terms of the stakes – to both the protagonist and antagonist.

The writer can feel comfortable not knowing all the details about this backstory. The important thing now is to know the structure know the story elements, and if the writer adheres to the model, the structure will fit into place, and the writer will be able to return to these details and fill them in later, knowing that they'll work into the story.

Cycle Three

Goals

The goal here is, naturally, that the superhero must safely extract Emily from this stronghold. What makes this goal feel fundamentally different than the Cycle Two goal is that the superhero's search was in the woods, which is a different setting than the town. A new set of obstacles and skills will need to be employed.

The singular question now is, "What will make the goal hard to achieve?" Given that prompt, the writer can start fleshing out what this stronghold is. What does it look like? How many people are here? Is this more of a *Mad Max*-style fortress, cobbled together with forest refuse, or a science-heavy laboratory where guards and scientists are bustling about?

At this point, it is sufficient to know that this environment should feel very different from the forest, and the goal should be hard in a new way. In this location, the superhero should feel surrounded by enemies in a way that he did not in the forest. He must employ skills of stealth (in the forest, he and his cohort were having to search and stay ahead of Mark) to sneak around this area and find Emily so they can extract her.

Failures

For the sake of variability, let's consider a different sort of failure for the superhero than in the first two cycles. This very thought process is one of the advantages of the GoFaSt model, as it allows the writer the ability to track their plot and character choices at important moments in the script. If it seems that some of the goals or failures are beginning to feel repetitive, this becomes plainly apparent, and new types of choices can be made.

If the first two failures saw the superhero unable to locate Emily, then let's have him locate her now. His failure must have come in a different way since failure does not always mean *not* achieving the goal – sometimes it means achieving the goal at a higher price than expected.

Perhaps the superhero could be gravely injured. Or Mark could somehow be emboldened when the superhero manages to save Emily. We have not developed the superhero's friend yet, but we have the placeholders for him to play an important role in the story. Knowing that we can go back and fill in the many blanks about who this character is, his backstory with the superhero, and his own arc – let's go ahead and doom the friend to die. The superhero saves Emily, but the friend dies in the process. Ideally, to keep the plot tidy, the friend dies in a similar way that the superhero caused the death of an innocent person in the opening scene. Not only does this choice help to bring full circle the superhero's relationship to his powers (perhaps in a moment of bitter irony, he had just become comfortable with his powers and was using them effectively to save Emily), but it brings back to the forefront that the superhero feels a dual within himself: he hates his powers, but he also needs them.

Stakes

Given the nature of this failure, what is at stake now is the superhero's very sense of identity. His relationship with himself, his mistakes, and his powers that so often go awry. More than the superhero's mere safety is at stake. Now, his nature is in question. He may be able to survive this story, but what kind of person will he become? The shift in stakes from issues of safety to those of identity will help to create a deeper layer to the story and increase its complexity as we head toward the end of the movie – the final, and the shortest, cycle.

Cycle Four

Goals

Given that each of these cycles feels to be around twenty or thirty script pages long, this cycle will be the final one – if this is to be a conventional feature film – and bring the total page count to around one hundred pages. Naturally, if we're feeling that there is more story to tell and we want to go longer, adding another cycle would be perfectly fine. The GoFaSt model is meant to give the writer flexibility to go longer if they feel the need or pull up short if the story seems to be reaching its natural conclusion.

With Emily safely found, the superhero's goal can write itself – if we like – and focus on a final confrontation with Mark. As we know from the first cycle, a superhero versus a regular human is not much of a match, and this would not be a hard goal. How can we make it harder? Perhaps the superhero is up against a small army of people from this area who are trying to stop him – Mark, his brothers, and other heavily armed folks. Conversely, if we want to explore the idea that this place has some origin story for the superhero's powers, then perhaps Mark can wield whatever technology is here and use powers of his own.

Either way – and there would be many other options as well – we're in a classic match-up of the antagonist versus the protagonist here, with plenty of room to throw in old grudges and pained feelings between Mark and Emily.

Failures

In the final cycle, we have an exception to the failure phase. Generally, if the movie is going to be a tragedy or end sadly, then the protagonist will encounter a final failure. However, if we want the protagonist to win and deliver a happy ending for audiences, then in the final cycle, failure is a win. The superhero can dispatch with Mark and escape this place with Emily.

Stakes

The final cycle gives us another exception for this stakes phase. The stakes here are often a summation of what this movie was about thematically. In defeating Mark, the superhero has come to terms with his power – a feeling of acceptance. The superhero is finally comfortable with his identity and the obligations and difficulties that come along with it.

Conclusion

The stakes of superhero movies are usually much bigger than in the sample storyline constructed in this exercise. What is at stake in recent Marvel and D.C. superhero films? The destruction of trains full of people, the safety of entire cities, or even the well-being of a planet or the whole universe. This makes sense for several reasons. One reason is that the profound gifts of superheroes – to fly, travel time, or exhibit enormous strength or intelligence – mean that they can achieve a great deal of good. If an ordinary person can be expected to save oneself or one's family, then an extraordinary person must be expected to save much more.

Another reason is that, due to the special effects required to produce these movies and the complex action sequences that audiences expect from them, superhero movies are expensive to make. Huge budgets mean that these movies will have to be seen as important events for commercial audiences, and it is natural to assume that big movies require big stakes. The bigger the stakes, the more important the movie feels. This logic is not entirely wrong.

However, it is also important to challenge the assumptions about the required ingredients of a superhero movie and to think about how this genre can remain nimble to continue to surprise and challenge audiences. All genres grow stale if the storytelling conventions remain rigid over time. The stakes part of the GoFaSt cycle is one place to potentially inspire a rethinking of this genre. What if, instead of going big, the stakes went more intimate? What would a superhero movie look like if the stakes of a drama were applied to the superhero's quest? Would this make the superhero more fleshed-out as a character? More tangible and identifiable to audiences? What do the stakes in this sample film say about the worldview of the protagonist?

As with the previous chapter's exercise on writing a horror movie, which considered changing the types of failures that its characters experience to update the haunted house sub-genre, this chapter looks – in part – and how different types of stakes can make the superhero film feel both familiar and different from what audiences traditionally expect to see.

References

Borzage, Frank (1927) *7th Heaven*. Fox Film Corporation.
Haynes, Todd (2019) *Joker*. Warner Bros.
Miller, George (1979) *Mad Max*. Roadshow Film.
Yan, Cathy (2020) *Birds of Prey*. Warner Bros.

The GoFaSt Guide to Screenwriting

7

GOFAST EXERCISE

Writing a Sample Heist Movie

Heist movies feature a character, or more often, a group of characters, stealing an object of value from a fortified or hard-to-reach place. These movies are often fun rides and feature a fast pace, clever characters, and nail-biting scenes of stealth. *Ocean's Eleven, Baby Driver,* and *Heat* are some of the highlights of the genre. Some amount of violence is also embedded within the expectations of the genre, and practitioners of the genre should be aware of the tricky line to draw, where these films often ask the audience to root for characters who sometimes injure or kill other characters. This is a similar challenge to gangster movies, which also usually see the protagonist, or main character, killing. Movies such as *The Godfather* and *The Sopranos* have long figured out how to help audiences excuse the very bad actions of the central characters. Sometimes the audience's sympathies are enshrined in a character by employing Blake Snyder's "save the cat" idea, where a character can act badly so long as they take one important action to show that – despite their misdeeds – they have a good (if troubled) heart. This is especially the case when the characters killed are the clear "bad guys" of the story.

However, another strategy seen in these films to garner audience sympathy for characters who behave badly is by establishing a strict code of ethics that the gangsters adhere to, which helps them seem not savage but just people who exist in a different set of rules than most. These dangerous protagonists do not commit random acts of chaos but instead live in a world that is merely harsher than ours and governed by codes of ethics. So long as the rules of this harsher world are clear and fair, and the protagonists struggle to adhere to them, the audience will have an easier time rooting for them. This is even

DOI: 10.4324/9781003141549-7

more true if the protagonist's actions ultimately rise to the values of our real world. For instance, in *The Godfather*, Michael Corleone is a sympathetic (though admittedly highly complex) character despite the killings he commits, because the killings are part of the course in mobster life and also – and more importantly – his killings are an effort to protect his father. This second point reflects the broader concerns and protocols of the real world in which the audience lives, and therefore, it is easier to root for him as he indulges in these shocking actions.

Heist films generally try to characterize the holders of the thing of value (that the protagonist is trying to steal) as either morally bankrupt or a faceless corporation. These characterizations can help heist movies overcome the bar of unacceptable moral behavior from a protagonist who may have to indulge in violent behavior to complete the heist.

This chapter will feature a writing exercise using the GoFaSt model to create the structure of a heist movie. To begin, we should first establish what is the thing of value that the main characters are hoping to steal. Money and artwork are common targets in this genre; banks and museums are exciting set pieces for the characters to sneak into, eluding security systems and eventually charging around in high-production-value sets with guns blazing. For the sake of fun, let's try something different.

Given the premise of this book being a screenplay, imagine that it's a screenplay being stolen. Screenplays can hold high value depending on who wrote them and the quality of the screenplay. Unlike cash or gold, which have inherent and immediate value, screenplays mostly have commercial value when in the hands of prominent filmmakers or actors. Cashing in on the value of a screenplay would be a niche and tricky action, but it is still possible. Who would want to steal a valuable screenplay, and who would have the ability to take advantage of the value of a particularly good one? Writers, of course. And more specifically, desperate writers.

We now have a target for our heist as well as a character or characters who will be the featured players driving the story. Does this mean that the valuable screenplay is the goal of the first cycle of our movie? Not necessarily. As discussed throughout this book, the goals should change and develop from one cycle to the next. If the ultimate goal of the movie is something other than stealing a screenplay, then the first goal might conceivably be the screenplay itself. However, if the climax of the film is the heist itself, then the first cycle should be something different. Also, given how unusual this target is, there will have to be plenty of stories to explain why a writer would want to steal a screenplay and what they could conceivably do with it. That might be too much exposition to load in the opening of a movie. Let's take our time getting there, and start with who these characters are.

Cycle One

Goals

Given that heist films often feature a group of characters and realizing that it can take several writers to write a script, let's say the first cycle will feature the main characters as two young, novice writers desperate to write a screenplay. Because these characters haven't yet read about the GoFaSt model, they're struggling to develop the story. They live in Los Angeles: college graduates who recently moved to strike it big in the film industry. Los Angeles is a place where writing can be hard because so many transplants share the same goals of fame and success. The sense of competition can be equal parts exhilarating and intimidating. Our two protagonists, feeling overwhelmed and stressed by a city jam-packed with aspiring screenwriters, decide they need to get away and clear their heads. They go to a resort town (Ojai is a popular nearby resort town) to get some writing done.

We now have a goal for the first cycle: to write a script. As previously discussed, one of the qualities of an effective goal is that it should be hard. As screenwriters, we can all agree that screenwriting is hard. But the goal should also have a determinate conclusion; that is, it should be clear that the goal has been either achieved or not achieved. One of the problems with "writing a screenplay" as a goal is that it takes very long to do, and because screenplays are often written, put away, and then re-engaged again for another draft (and many times over again), it can be hard to know whether the goal has been achieved or failed.

We'll need to add an element to the goal, to have it comply with the necessary characteristics. Ticking clocks are useful for making goals definable. Let's say that the script needs to be completed in a week (perhaps they've already been working on it for some time and already have a rough draft), and there is an interested producer who has set this deadline. If our two writers can finish it in a week, this producer can find the financing to get the movie made. After a week, the financing goes away. Perhaps this producer has come along to Ojai, along with an actor who's attached to the movie. The four of them together will work on completing the final draft.

With the goal in place, an added element to definitively determine success or failure (the deadline of one week), and four protagonists, this first cycle of the script is beginning to take shape. For the sake of providing some focus within this ensemble cast, let's also make one of these writers the main character of the foursome: Erin, a talented writer who lacks confidence but has plenty of ambition and boldness to give her a reasonable shot at success.

Failures

The most obvious failure here is that the writing team fails to write the script. Is this failure interesting enough? It depends on exactly how they fail.

First, while goals should be simple and clear, failures benefit from complexity and unexpectedness. A worthwhile activity is to think about just how terribly wrong the goal could go – what are the most outrageous ways that the writing team could fail? In real life, scripts usually fail by the idea fizzling out or the writer losing interest. This is not terribly cinematic. A better reason for the failure will have to be considered.

Second, a week (if that's the deadline we're sticking with) is a long time for the audience to wait for the failure to be realized. That's a lot of bad writing sessions to get through before they miss the deadline.

So, perhaps there's a more interesting and complicated way that they could fail at the goal. In-fighting between the foursome is more interesting than bad, or unproductive, writing sessions. The producer is perhaps bullying and demanding; the actor maybe gets sidetracked from the writing to pursue an old lover in Ojai or parties too hard and winds up in jail, and the producer must bail him out. Their lives are all too chaotic and their personalities too difficult for them to figure out how to work together.

The failure, then, is not missing the deadline but rather everyone splitting up like a self-destructive indie rock band. Screaming and hilarious arguments. A hotel room getting trashed. An arrogant actor sitting in jail for the night. Egos and terrible ideas abound, and the goal ends with each character booking tickets to head back home to Los Angeles. They swear to never see one another again.

Naturally, through all this chaos, which could be quite fun to watch, it would still be important to offer the audience a morsel of belief in these characters. Despite their many flaws, there is a spark of creativity that were they to get along, and be able to communicate and focus, perhaps they could do something great. The audience should want to hope that there is something worthwhile in these characters – especially Erin, in whom the audience sees the most promise – such that the audience would be able to root for their success.

Stakes

What is at stake are the dreams of these young hopefuls. Seeing them give up on the reason that they came to Los Angeles, and aspired to live as filmmakers, would be painful and disappointing. Their pursuits must feel authentic and derive from a place of honest ambition and creative desire, for the audience to be concerned about these stakes.

Cycle Two

Goals

What goal could revive the writing team's hopes? A new element would have to come into the story, which would allow for a new goal to emerge. Given the genre that we're embarking on, here is where the heist can be introduced. What could they steal that would help them realize their dreams? A screenplay. A very valuable screenplay. What makes a screenplay valuable? Perhaps it is written by a famous writer. One could imagine a goal where they have uncovered some brilliant, unproduced script by Orson Welles or Billy Wilder.

However, one of the advantages of starting a new cycle is that each cycle represents an opportunity to bring new elements into the story, such as a big event that affects the lives of the characters, or a new character. This new character could be an antagonist (since this story does not yet have one) who is the writer of the valuable screenplay.

Here's how such a scene may work: on their last day before leaving town, the foursome is bitter and not talking to each other. They sit at a café in silence, ordering breakfast and coffee before heading to the airport. The producer of the team happens to notice that they're at the same café as a famous screenwriter – our new antagonist. Everyone is in awe for a moment, as this screenwriter (let's call him Andre) has written some of the biggest blockbusters in recent years. He is famously secretive about his scripts and has a famously difficult and distasteful personality. There are also rumors that he's made a fortune stealing other writers' ideas. Andre lives the kind of success that they could only dream of, but he's also a terrible person.

As everyone watches Andre, the producer notices an interesting quirk: Andre is ordering a chocolate mousse for himself to be baked for tomorrow. The producer – based on this observation – tells the others that it appears Andre has just finished a new screenplay. Everyone wonders how he knows this, and the producer says he read an interview that Andre writes in total secrecy, and when his new script is finished and ready to sell, he eats a chocolate mousse to celebrate prior to showing the script to his agent.

The writing team is impressed by this knowledge. They also make two observations. First, Andre's laptop is sitting casually on the table with the screenplay up on his screen as he taps away at the last edits. Second, Andre treats the staff at the café very rudely. He is the antagonist, after all, and to maintain some easy audience sympathy for the foursome, Andre should be as despicable as possible. The four protagonists joke about sneaking a peek at the script for some ideas on their own, faltering screenplay – and then advance the joke by suggesting that they steal his script. Given his terrible treatment of other people, they feel justified in doing this. Since Andre never shows his scripts to anyone until they are complete (and he's eaten his ritualistic chocolate mousse), they could take the script and claim it as their own.

On a whim, they decide to do this: steal Andre's script. They deserve some success, and Andre deserves some comeuppance for all his previous bad behaviors. As they agree to do this, Andre packs up his laptop and leaves the café. If they are to steal his screenplay, they have until tomorrow to do it (because after he shows it to his agent, it will be impossible to claim that they actually wrote the script).

This goal is certainly hard, as all goals should be. Perhaps Andre is staying at a fancy hotel with security. They will need to find his hotel and his room number and manage to get inside. There are plenty of opportunities to plot high-jinks, character conflict, and development for the four protagonists as the ticking clock nears and their desperation grows. Perhaps the writers must write a great script that will convince the security guards to let them in, and the actor realizes (in evading the security system) that he has action-star skills in real life. The act of planning and performing the heist allows them to learn important information about themselves.

Failures

The writing team failing to get the script is the most obvious type of failure they could experience, but we should brainstorm the most interesting way that this might happen. They could retrieve the laptop but then accidentally destroy it in the process. Another idea is that they might be caught and arrested by the police. Once in jail, they would have to figure out how to get bailed out and then conceive of an entirely different approach to getting the script. Yet another idea is that Andre himself could capture them and publicly humiliate them thereby destroying their chances of getting the script, and possibly ending their careers.

In deciding which direction to take (one of the above or many other ideas that we could consider), it is important to determine which idea might cause the most complications and be the most dire to their safety and outcomes. Which failure is the most visual? Which failure feels the most unique and unconventional, according to audience expectations? Part of the genius of the Coen brothers, as previously mentioned, is how spectacularly their protagonists fail. How creatively original and narratively complex the failures are. Goals create energy and momentum in a script, yes, but failures are narrative playgrounds for writers to write the most fun, tragic, or exciting scenes for the audience to experience – depending on the genre and tone of the movie.

Another consideration is to make this failure as personal as possible. Perhaps Andre's security catches the foursome and holds them under house arrest. Andre humiliates them and takes joy in their suffering and creative frustrations. He could assure them of how talentless they are, and how unattainable their dreams are. Then he makes them watch as he opens his script on the laptop, saves it as a PDF, and emails the script to his agent. The ticking clock has expired – with the agent seeing the script from Andre, there is now no chance they could steal it and claim it as their own.

Stakes

The stakes here are more personal than in the previous cycle. Whereas in that cycle, their dreams were at stake, now Andre's defeat of them is so pointed that they are forced to doubt themselves entirely. Doubt whether they have any talent. It is their core self-esteem that is at stake.

If Andre goes public with their scheme – perhaps he takes their pictures and posts the photographs on social media, with a claim that they tried to steal his script – then potentially their ability to work again in the industry is also at stake.

Cycle Three

Goals

The analyses of *Mrs. Maisel* and *Portrait of a Lady on Fire* (in later chapters in this book) show that sometimes the goals from one cycle to the next can repeat, provided that a new plot element is introduced to make the new goal slightly different. Let's try that here.

The foursome has not only failed at their goal of stealing the script, but Andre has also put them on social media blasting as thieves. Things could not be worse for them. In the traditional three-act structure, this late-in-the-script failure is sometimes referred to as the big gloom – a situation so bleak that it is impossible for the audience to think of a way that the protagonists might somehow succeed or survive their predicament.

Andre has let the four people go free and heads off to the café to eat his chocolate mousse. Defeated and deflated, they start heading back to Los Angeles – and, quite likely, back to the hometowns where they're from to start different careers. But Erin stops them – she still wants to steal Andre's laptop. The others balk at this – it doesn't matter anymore because the script is now in the agent's hands. But Erin insists she has an idea of how to still emerge victorious. They refuse to help, so Erin decides that she will go it alone: she will steal Andre's laptop on her own.

This goal is the same as the second cycle, but it's different, because now we have a lone character trying to pull off the impossible and because she has a secret agenda that could still work in everyone's favor.

A new cycle is a prime opportunity to introduce a new character, story element, or location. So, let's do that here and bring the story back to

Los Angeles, where Andre lives. Erin might team up with someone in LA to achieve this goal – an old lover or a roommate – and the two of them endeavor to locate Andre and his laptop. This goal is hard, in part, because of the public scorn that Erin faces at every turn.

Nevertheless, Erin eventually locates Andre and steals his laptop. This being the final cycle of this script, the action required (we're only writing the structure here and therefore don't yet need to spell out all the narrative steps taken) should top what was seen in the second cycle's attempts to take the laptop. After a great deal of work and effort, Erin has the laptop in her hands and gathers the foursome to open Andre's screenplay document in front of everyone.

Failures

The final cycle's failure is, for a movie that has a happy ending (as this one does), not a failure but rather a success. Erin opens the laptop, and everyone sees that Andre's script is, in fact, the script that the four of them had been working on but failed to complete. Andre – whose theft of other writers' ideas has long been suspected – actually stole their idea when they came to Ojai. During the time that the foursome was fighting and arguing about the script, Andre was busy writing it to completion.

Because the writers had emailed their drafts to their producers, they have proof that they wrote these pages of the script (or at least, an earlier draft of it) prior to Andre's email to the agent. With this proof in hand, the foursome can confront Andre's agent, and soon they will be exonerated by the public of Andre's charges against them. Even better, with all the attention on them, their script now has the heat to make a big sale in the Hollywood marketplace.

Stakes

Given the reveal that Andre stole the foursome's rough draft, the theme of this movie is believing in oneself. The four protagonists realize that they're good writers – good enough for the biggest writer in Hollywood to steal their idea. Achieving their dreams did not depend on their lack of ability, it turns out, but on their willingness to trust their talents and hard work.

Conclusion

The previous two chapters used the GoFaSt model to identify specific aspects of a script that can be changed to make old genres feel fresh. For instance, in the horror genre, we looked at what happens when the types of failures that the characters experience vary from conventional choices. A similar approach was done to the superhero genre, by examining what happens when the stakes of our superhero story are different than the conventional ones.

In this chapter, we look at the heist genre and consider giving unconventional goals to the protagonists. What if, instead of wanting gold or the contents of a bank safe, the protagonists wanted a screenplay? How would this impact an audience's expectations for the genre, and how would the action play out differently than what most heist movies would see? Instead of guns and ski masks, this movie would feature computers and passwords. Instead of banks and hidden warehouses, this movie would take place in a resort town and a writer's retreat.

By re-imagining these goals, the basic structure of the genre remains similar to the well-trodden and successful conventions that many other heist movies have used, but the story is new and different. Breaking down a script into cycles of goals, failures, and stakes allows a writer to not only uncover the possibilities of their own script but to also look at other movies and find places to make new choices, to write something original and personal that is inspired by past films but forward-looking to what current audiences want to see.

References

Coppola, Francis Ford (1972) *The Godfather*. Paramount Pictures.
Mann, Michael (1995) *Heat*. Warner Bros.
Sciamma, Celine (2019) *Portrait of a Lady on Fire*. Pyramide Films.
Soderbergh, Steven (2001) *Ocean's Eleven*. Warner Bros.
Wright, Edgar (2017) *Baby Driver*. Sony Pictures.

The GoFaSt Guide to Screenwriting

8

GOFAST CASE STUDY

There Will Be Blood

There are four case studies in this book. Each case study illustrates how the GoFaSt model operates in different formats of writing for the screen – such as feature films or episodic – as well as a variety of implementations of the model. That is to say, these case studies will not merely replicate the same information across four examples but also highlight the flexibility of the model and how it can be used in a variety of structural narrative situations. GoFaSt is a model designed to allow for maximum flexibility; it looks and behaves differently in different stories, genres, styles of writing, and formats of screen storytelling. It is a model that embraces a certain amount of messiness and eccentricity in how the screenwriter wants to tell the story. By loosening the grip on the steering wheel of screenplay structure, as it were, GoFaSt allows for more fluid racing – to continue the metaphor – and more impulsive acts of improvisational or gestured writing. It is meant to make screenwriters feel empowered by exploring their creative impulses, and not constricted by what they are "allowed" or "not allowed" to do while maintaining narrative cohesion.

   Models that advocate for more strictness – such as the specific page-count rules set in place by Blake Snyder's *Save the Cat* – can be extremely useful, and for writers who feel terrifically lost in a story and require more discipline, these models are wonderful to have. Additionally, writers may need different requirements for their models at different stages of the writing process. Some writers may need a more "fill in the blanks" approach when outlining the major events of their scripts, or they may need a more buttoned-down model later in the process to help align the narrative details of their scripts to achieve the necessary efficiency in the pacing of the story. Many of these advantages are explored in the earlier interviews in the book.

DOI: 10.4324/9781003141549-8

This book merely advocates permission for writers to be able to jump from one model to the next, for the writer to be able to pick-and-choose, since – practically speaking – this is the approach many contemporary professional writers use. And the previous interviews show examples of how this is done responsibly – when it works and when it doesn't. This book also offers the GoFaSt model as an option that weighs toward flexibility and allows for a more gesture-driven writing style, where screenwriters can be less rule-bound while having enough organizational power to keep their stories moving along proficiently. If a screenwriter is allowed to sometimes meander, detour, and experiment – even in the finished script, and the finished film – while maintaining a strong story structure, then often the film is better. The lists of filmmakers who leave behind narrative structural rigidness and embrace a certain amount of meandering but are nevertheless strong in structure in a more organic way are long. The Coen Brothers, Kelly Reichardt, and Asghar Farhadi are some of the names of on endlessly long list of filmmakers who tell these types of well-structured, organic, meandering, and wonderfully quirky stories. These writers would never be described as free-form in their structural approach, but they are also not classicists when it comes to writing.

This chapter's case study focuses on a notoriously unwieldy and eccentric script: *There Will Be Blood*, written by Paul Thomas Anderson and based on the Upton Sinclair novel, *Oil!* The movie is also directed by Anderson and filmed with an eye toward the grandiose cinemas of David Lean and John Ford and the psychologically terrifying art house/commercial crossover oeuvre of the likes of William Friedkin.

One of the many appealing reasons to use *There Will Be Blood* as a case study is that we have both the script and finished movie authored by the same person, which offers a highly complete rendition of his vision of the story. As such, this chapter will shift back-and-forth between the script (here, using the popularly available July 25, 2006 "pink draft") and the film itself to illustrate Anderson's telling of his story. To get the most information out of this chapter, it will be useful for the reader to be familiar with both the script and the movie. However, as a primer, here is a summary of *There Will Be Blood*. These are the basic beats of the film, to aid the following discussion. Beware: spoilers abound.

There Will Be Blood

Daniel Plainview, the protagonist of this film, is a prospector. The movie opens with him in the deserts of the American Southwest, searching for silver. The year is 1898, and he is deep inside a mine shaft working with the rough and dangerous tools of his trade, among them a pickaxe and dynamite, to extract the precious ore. An accident with the dynamite leaves him with a broken leg, or ankles, as described in the script, and barely able to drag himself away from the mine and across the desert floor toward civilization. Nevertheless, he perseveres and sells his silver. This small fortune leads him into the more profitable business of drilling for oil, and – after acquiring an infant boy named HW when a worker dies – Daniel eventually arrives in a California town called Little Boston, where he begins leasing land to establish an oil well of potentially staggering monetary value.

Eli, a self-serving pastor in Little Boston whose ambitions for growing his congregation and church, sees in Daniel's arrival both a threat to his influence over the local population and an opportunity for wealth. Eli embarks on a contentious and complex relationship with Daniel. Meanwhile, HW befriends a local girl named Mary (Eli's young sister), whose father abuses her – much to the chagrin of Daniel. When HW is injured and loses his hearing, Daniel sends him out of town in a brutal scene of abandonment, and Daniel happenstance meets a man named Henry who claims to be Daniel's brother.

As Henry's dim-wittedness and indulgences drag Daniel down, Eli seems to gain a foothold in his battles with Daniel. Eventually, the oil derrick strikes pay dirt, Daniel becomes enormously wealthy, and the film cuts to twenty years in the future. Daniel is now a very wealthy man living in a mansion, alone and half-crazy. HW, a grown man, returns to Daniel to bring closure to their relationship. But when Daniel learns that HW is going into the oil business, Daniel sends him away, claiming to have never loved him. Eli subsequently comes to visit Daniel, and after the two men discuss old wounds and Eli reveals his desperation for money, Daniel kills him with demented glee.

Beginnings and Endings

In most feature-length scripts, there will be three GoFaSt cycles. The number of cycles is unimportant if their integrity is sound. Longer scripts might have more cycles, and if the cycles are shorter in length, then a script with an average page count might have more cycles as well.

There is also a beginning and an ending to every script that sets up the cycles and, subsequently, concludes them. In the context of this model, beginnings and endings are conceptually straightforward events that mostly need to achieve a single requirement to successfully get the script going. The beginning and ending can be looked at simply as a *question* that is fundamental to the protagonist and then an *answer* to that question.

The Question

In the opening pages of *There Will Be Blood*, one possible question raised is this: given all the challenges that Daniel will experience in the initial sequences (broken leg, death of a co-worker, and now having to care for a child in the desert), how will he succeed as a prospector? Part of the success of a script depends on the quality of the question posed by the screenwriter and the inventiveness and creativity of the answer. There are many ways to frame the opening question, and one might think that a more obvious question posed by the script might be this: *will* Daniel succeed? But this is less interesting than *how* will Daniel succeed, because *will* he succeed merely sets up the script for a yes or no answer. How surprising can the ending of the movie be when there is only one of two options available to the writer? A better question is needed.

Additionally, Anderson sets up Daniel as a force of nature. He is not merely a man with a dream for success but a hard worker looking to capitalize on the free market advantages of a burgeoning American industry by digging in a mineral-rich area of unspoiled land. That is not the story Anderson wants to tell. This is not *Hoosiers* or a story of an underdog seeking to make good. That type of story has nothing to do with Anderson's grander, darker vision of a man who will, no doubt, make good but will accumulate casualties along the way of his success. Daniel is demonic, almost supernatural in his ability to suffer, to work, and to create wealth and followers from mere dirt. *Will he* has nothing to do with the boldness of the story Anderson seeks to tell or the power of the character he has created.

How implies a process – a series of steps that the protagonist must take. *How* implies that the character's success may not even be what we – as the audience – necessarily want. *How* is also – specifically in this story – a better question than *why*, because *how* makes the protagonist inherently active. *Will* is somewhat more passive and suggests that the answer will be placed upon the protagonist, not just by his own work or the sweat of his brow, but also by fortune or fate. In F. Scott Fitzgerald's famous notation that "character is action," we know that by creating the need and room in the story for a process to occur (as opposed to a yes or no final judgment), then the writer has put themselves in a position where they can create the character not through description or backstory but through taking steps from one point to another. The process shows how the character thinks, it shows their moral framework (what actions they're willing to take and what actions they won't), and it shows the level of their fortitude, and it puts them in a position of having to make decisions.

The right question is needed to begin the first cycle of the script. *How* is frequently a strong word to incorporate into the question. Mysteries often ask *who* the killer is (think whodunnits), but with audiences becoming savvier and more aware – if not tired – of a few tropes of the genre, some more contemporary movies seek to throw the audience on a new ride. For instance, *Knives Out* puts a clever twist by asking *who* at first, only to reveal the answer to that question surprisingly early in the film, and then rephrasing the question to *how* – as in, *how* will the central character Marta not get caught for a crime that the audience already believes she committed? The journalistic advice about writing articles to answer the 5 Ws and 1 H – Who What When Where Why and How? – are valid, but the *how* is often the most vital in most cases. It is clearly not the only best question to put at the start of the script, but the more that the screenwriter can skew the question into an action-based, process-oriented framing of the opening question, the more material they likely may have to play with as the cycles begin.

The Answer

If the screenwriter's question should usually not be binary and should suggest a process and a wide-open landscape upon which to let the answer play out, what makes a great answer? The answer – which comes at the end of the script – should not avoid the question. This doesn't mean that the ending should be clear and wrapped up, but it also shouldn't be vague. No one likes when a question is avoided. A concise answer can still be deliciously ambiguous. Ambiguity is effective and tantalizing for audiences because it allows for interpretations and post-movie discussions. Vagueness, on the other hand, suggests a script that is uncertain of its own plotting.

Well-conceived answers can be disarming, scary, unexpected, and unexpectedly honest. These are all ways to describe a great ending to a story. The answer does not need to be figured out before writing in earnest begins. The answer can come to the writer as they write. To lose sight of the question risks putting the writer in the position of writing an ending that does not deliver on expectations. Or seems random or forced. Writing a script is an interview between a writer and themselves, with a question and an answer discussing the protagonist.

The GoFaSt Cycles

In between the question and answer in the script are the GoFaSt cycles. The cycles lead the story from the question to create the circumstances in which the answer may arrive. Unlike the three-act structure, which limits the script to three acts told in a specific order, GoFaSt makes room for scripts to have variety in the number of cycles, depending on the length of the script and the pacing of the story. Longer scripts will likely have more cycles; faster-paced thrill-a-minute scripts will also likely have more (though shorter) cycles.

There Will Be Blood is a long script, but also one that moves at a meticulous pace. It retains enormous power in its pacing. Watching it is like watching an industry develop, history play itself out, or geology change. I see three cycles in the script. Looking at each of them in order shows the GoFaSt model at work.

Cycle One

How will Daniel succeed as an oil man? To answer that question, let's look at Daniel's initial efforts to build a derrick. Early in the script, Daniel meets a young pastor named Eli, who sells information about an area of land (set in the fictional California town of Little Boston) that may have abundant subterranean reserves of oil. Daniel visits the town and begins leasing land and constructing a derrick. The goal is well-established, clear to the audience, and – as one would want with any goal – actionable. That is, the goal is not something amorphous, such as the protagonist wants to be happy or wants spiritual fulfillment. These kinds of goals do not inspire specific actions or create the circumstances for a viable antagonist.

Goals

Daniel arrives in Little Boston with one objective: to find oil. To do this, he needs land, workers, and the consent of locals, and he must build a derrick. These are all specific challenges that can be achieved by the protagonist taking specific actions. We see Daniel urging and intimidating real estate agent Al Rose to buy enormous swaths of land, finding contractors to build roads and dig wells, placating Eli, who wants to assert a spiritual domain over the work at the derrick, while also domineering over Eli's father Abel to underman his authority over his own family and, ostensibly, in town.

In this early section of the first cycle, Daniel is hard at work, and the advantage of having such a specific goal is that we get to know him through action. The disdain he shows for Al, the caution he shows toward Eli and Abel (initially, at least), and the chiding respect he shows for fellow prospector Gene display a character who is multi-faceted, intelligent, observant, and dangerous.

Another advantage of having the protagonist operate in such a goal-driven fashion is that the pacing of the story never lags. How could it be, when Daniel is constantly in motion? If Daniel and the script do not lose sight of this goal, then the scenes of him working to achieve it have relevance and pacing for the larger narrative structure.

Failures

Failure comes in many different stripes. Most frequently, failure means that the protagonist does not achieve their goal. They try, but one or more of the obstacles that they face overwhelms them, or the protagonist loses motivation or suffers an injury, such that the goal is lost. The protagonist will head into the next cycle with a new goal, usually related to the first goal, to try again to achieve what they need – and answer the original question of the script. If the script can keep a focus on this original question and not lose sight of it, then the cycles have more flexibility in terms of the narrative ground that they cover or the directions that they go without the script feeling lost or rambling. Set the anchor of the original question, and the ship has room to move with the waves as it sees fit.

However, in other cases of failure – and as is the case in *There Will Be Blood* – the protagonist will succeed at the goal but wind up paying an unexpected price for that success. Paying too much for success is a type of effective and dramatic failure. Daniel builds the derrick, but when the derrick finally produces oil after months of speculation and setbacks, it is rocked by a massive explosion of gas and liquid. Daniel's son, HW, who had been sitting on the derrick and watching the workers working the derrick, was badly injured in the explosion. His body goes flying, and he hits his head, causing him to go deaf. This condition is revealed to be permanent. Daniel's reaction to his son's injury is complex, with the father at times showing enormous tragic emotion and at other times reacting callously. But the injury does leave Daniel devastated in his own, twisted way, and he eventually chooses to send the boy away to live at a school for the deaf.

Daniel's derrick has come in, but he's lost his son in the bargain. In the failure stage of the cycle, if the goal is achieved, then the price paid is often a higher value than the goal itself. Whether Daniel values his son over his wealth is a subject of debate in this movie, and the complexity of Daniel's character ensures that an answer is not entirely clear; regardless, however, we do see enormous pain in his character at times, and the price is significant. Significant enough, in fact, to establish the foundation for the goal of the second cycle. But before we get to that cycle, let's look at the stakes of the first.

Stakes

The third stage of the cycle concerns the stakes of the story. As a result of the failure, the stakes should change for the protagonist. When stakes are usually discussed in scripts, it is commonly believed that the stakes should increase. This is not always the case. Sometimes, the stakes grow more intimate. In the beginning of the movie *Wall-E*, the health of planet Earth is at stake. At the end of the movie, the well-being and habitability of the Earth are still at play, but the stakes have ultimately grown smaller: the main character Wall-E is not just fighting for the planet; he is fighting for his love of Eve. Certainly, the planet is "bigger" than his relationship with Eve, but stakes are relative – and they should be – and so the love with Eve feels enormous to us by the end. One needs only to look at Italian neo-realist films to see that smaller stakes can feel enormously consequential as long as they matter to characters about whom we care (such as finding the stolen bicycle in *Bicycle Thieves*); the same goes for the cinema of Abbas Kiarostami, in films such as *Where is the Friend's House?*, where a boy delivering a notebook to a schoolmate becomes of extraordinary importance. In the world of stakes, bigger is certainly not always better.

Either way, whether the stakes grow objectively larger or more intimate, the point is, they should evolve to maintain the audience's attention. Some movies begin with stakes maximized in terms of objective size from the very start of the movie but then do not change, and no matter how big those stakes initially are, it inevitably grows tiresome for the audience. No stakes are big enough to sustain – in their original form – the audience's attention for an entire film.

Additionally, it is important for the stakes to change because this third stage of the cycle is what prevents the script from becoming episodic. Screen stories are more than – or should be more than – a series of events befalling a protagonist. The screw needs to tighten as the narrative progresses. The audience should lean forward as they watch. The realities of the outside world should fall further away as the story nears its end. These things are achieved by a writer controlling the stakes. The stakes put pom-poms in the hands of the audience and told us when to cheer, how hard to cheer, and for whom. The stakes help us – the audience – worry for a character, root for a character, feel a knot in our stomachs over the well-being of the character – essentially, all those emotional responses one hopes to inspire from an audience. Stakes give the story dimension and depth, emotional resonance, and a feeling of building inertia.

In this first cycle, the stakes for Daniel are this: his fortune was at stake at the beginning of the cycle, and now his son's health is at stake. How does the change in stakes deepen the story? It expands the range of themes that the film addresses beyond greed and industry, which are introduced early on. The audience can feel involved in a character's financial investment in a project, but as the narrative moves forward, no amount of money can keep our interest. So, the stakes shift toward the personal – the familial – and become not bigger but more intimate. Now, his son's health is what's on the chopping block.

By the end of this cycle, the failure and shift in stakes, brings the story to a new phase and a new direction. The cycles should relate to each other, each setting up the subsequent either with regards to theme, plot, character, or the many other strands upon which a narrative is built. This is the function of the "bridges" referred to in the metaphor earlier in this chapter. And this is one of the flexible aspects of the GoFaSt model because it allows the writer to pick up a strand that they are excited by or that is unexpected and use that to continue the story. The writer should not feel hamstrung to stay in a particular lane or direction. Using one's own ideas as jumping-off points for a new phase in the story can help to create scripts that are organically designed, unexpected, and – if they do not move randomly from one cycle to the next – logically designed.

Cycle Two

Looking back to the original question of the script – how will Daniel succeed? – the second cycle sees Daniel approaching the question from a new angle. His efforts have brought in the gushing well, but he has lost his son in the process. Given the context of this story – nineteenth-century American industry – when so many family dynasties were built, such as the Rockefellers and Vanderbilts, it makes sense that Daniel needs a family to help handle and develop his business. As a paranoid, angry man who does not get along with others, family is really his only choice as far as anyone whom he could trust and would be willing to stick by him. As an unmarried, private man whose sole obsession is work, his efforts to create a family are naturally hindered. He has, most importantly, lost his son.

Ironically, the script paints Daniel as a man who has trouble creating a traditional family, but he is a masterfully successful father figure from a mythic perspective. Early in the film, we see him obtain a baby almost from thin air in the middle of the desert when the baby's biological father is killed in a drilling accident. Later in Little Boston, Daniel usurps Mary's father – who abuses the girl – and buys her a dress and threatens the father to not beat her anymore. Daniel becomes a sort of *uber*-father figure, and yet he is unable to act as or be a true father.

Goals

A few pages after HW's injury, a stranger appears at Daniel's cottage, waiting for him to return home from the derrick. The stranger, Henry, identifies himself as Daniel's long-lost half-brother. He carries documentation (a letter from Daniel's sister, Anabelle) that supposedly proves his identity, but his origins are mysterious, and Daniel is hesitant to trust the man. HW, now deaf because of the injury and still living at the cottage, also seems to distrust the man and, in a fit of frustration, attempts to burn down their cottage. Daniel acts out of a complicated series of motivations and sends his son, unwilling to leave his father, out of town.

There are multiple possible readings of this event. On the one hand, Daniel knows that he cannot help his son recover in this makeshift oil town – the medical resources are simply not here – so he is sending HW to northern California, where he can find the help that he needs. On the other hand, because of HW's condition, some viewers credibly offer that Daniel no longer has use for HW. As a prop of the family business – who could serve as a cute mascot in Daniel's meetings, a symbol that Daniel was to be trusted – HW is now less valuable, and so Daniel discards him. With Henry stepping into Daniel's life as a sort of replacement for HW, Daniel is able to shift his vision for the expansion of a family business to Henry.

This alliance with Henry defines the scope and direction of the second cycle's goal. Daniel needs Henry because Daniel needs an heir. We see this goal play out in scenes where Daniel starts bringing Henry to important business meetings, instead of George – Daniel's previous trusted aide. We also see Daniel testing Henry and adjudicating whether to bring this man into the business. These are all actions that support the primary goal of this cycle. Judging by Henry's defeated demeanor and quiet presence in meetings, and his personal indiscretions, Henry appears to be less reliable than George. And yet Daniel chooses Henry, blinded by his goal of familial business expansionism.

Failures

Approximately thirty script pages pass until Daniel encounters his failure. During a scene at a beach when Henry seems to have no recollection of a childhood memory that, if he were related to Daniel, would be shared. Daniel suspects that Henry has lied about his identity and eventually confronts him, holding a gun on Henry and forcing a confession. When Henry reveals that Daniel's real half-brother is dead, even though by no foul play by Henry, Daniel shoots Henry dead and buries the body. Daniel's goal to expand the family has been met with failure. His real brother – whose identity Henry had stolen, turns out to have previously died from an illness. Given Daniel's increasing wariness – and even hatred – of other people and his advancing age, his chances of establishing a family for his dynasty are growing ever slimmer. Henry was his last hope.

Once Henry is gone, Daniel's aloneness in this world becomes staggering; his increasingly self-imposed isolation is complete. He hates everyone, he says. His *uber*-fatherly mythic qualities are gone, and he has turned into someone who would rather kill those around him than accumulate any new contacts, familial or otherwise. Not that he ever openly states this desire, but the desire is implicit, and Daniel will never be a Vanderbilt or a Rockefeller. His oil business begins and ends with his own life; there will be no heir.

Stakes

The morning after Henry's murder, Daniel is woken by Bandy, the grizzled old-timer whose land Daniel had been hoping to lease for building a pipeline. Bandy, a religious follower of Eli, demands that Daniel be baptized by Eli in exchange for granting the lease. Bandy presents Daniel with evidence of the murder he has committed, and because of this evidence, for the first time that we have seen in the movie, Daniel is in a vulnerable position. He has been successfully blackmailed. He is a murderer whose fate no longer rests with his own power and wherewithal – he has been subjugated under the will and desire of someone else's agenda. This is a riskier position for Daniel than any other time in the movie.

What is new at stake for Daniel by the end of the second cycle? His own agency. His freedom. As a murderer, with testimony and evidence against him (the gun that Bandy found, not to mention the crudely buried body in a shallow grave), Daniel could conceivably go to jail. He can no longer press every other character under his thumb by using intimidation and threat; now, he is under someone else's thumb. He must act in accordance with another's commands: here, the religious commands of Bandy. Daniel's vulnerability shifts the story into a new narrative territory: the third cycle.

Cycle Three

The third cycle of *There Will Be Blood* showcases the flexibility built into the GoFaSt model. After the failure of the second goal, Daniel's obsession turns to building a pipeline to transport his oil for sale. The derrick has been a success in terms of the amount of oil it has produced, but this success has cost him his son, and furthermore, it has cost him any chance at a familial legacy. Alone in the world now with nothing but his wealth and what he describes as "an ocean of oil" beneath his feet, he needs to find a way to transport the oil for sale. This goal will bring to close a logical sequence of events that the story has laid out – start a business, expand a business, and become rich from the business.

What is particularly fascinating in this third cycle is that the goal is introduced early in the script. In fact, by page 26, all three goals have been established. If the goal is introduced in the first act and the actions taken don't occur until act three, does that mean the cycle is over a hundred pages long? No. One of the intriguing aspects of this model is that the three phases of a cycle don't necessarily need to be linear. The goals are lighthouses set out across the nighttime ocean, but they don't need to be set in a row. The bridges that link them don't have to be straight. A goal can be established early, and then failures seeded over the course of dozens of pages, and the failure and stakes delivered later. As long as the cycle remains intact – even segmented out across the course of a script – the plot can retain its structural integrity.

This option for a deferment of one or the other stages of a cycle allows the writer to control the pacing of the story. If the plot is tumbling forth too fast, then a subplot can be introduced to bring the audience into another narrative arena until the pacing feels right to return to the cycle.

Goals

The goal of the first cycle is established when Daniel is first scouting the oil prospects in Little Boston with his son. Daniel states that they will need to pump the oil through a pipeline to sell it; otherwise, he says, "It's just mud." This goal comes up in subsequent conversations with Al Rose as it relates to leasing land, and then again in the argument with the representatives from Standard Oil, H.M. Tilford, and J.J. Carter, when Daniel accuses them of illegally controlling the costs of shipping oil.

The goal of the third cycle is clear: build a pipeline. There are scenes of Daniel working toward this goal, but these scenes are scattered throughout much of the script. They come up on occasion, operating more like a subplot than a central goal. But when the second cycle completes, those previous scenes have set up for the third cycle to jump straight into action. Anderson can quickly start this third cycle without spending much time explaining the purpose or circumstances of the goal – indeed, they have already been established. The pacing is excellent, as the audience is shoved directly from the stakes of the second cycle into the failure of the third cycle.

Failures

The characteristics of this cycle's failure resemble that of the first cycle in that Daniel does achieve his goal, but this success comes at a higher cost than he expected. To win the lease, he must be baptized by Eli. Believing this ceremony to be something minor, a mere annoyance to be briefly endured, Daniel finds himself – during the baptism – taunted by Eli in front of the congregation. When Daniel is forced to admit that he abandoned his child by sending the stricken boy away on a train, Daniel must confront the ugliness of what he has done. The emotional wreckage of his surprisingly honest and profoundly emotional confessional pierces the screen with Daniel Day Lewis's extraordinary performance. Daniel, the character, must reveal – in front of a packed congregation – his weaknesses and shortcomings. The moment is a dramatic earthquake.

Furthermore, in a daring spectacle of opportunism, Eli takes advantage of Daniel's breakdown (as well as his physical posturing since Daniel is down on his knees during the baptism) to slap Daniel in the face. Several times. This act is certainly in retaliation for a previous beating that Daniel had given Eli. Daniel is publicly humiliated in a fashion that had been inconceivable for most of the film. It is this slapping, this humiliation, and especially the emotional resonance of the confession that marks Daniel's failure in this cycle and sets up for the final scenes of his lonely self-destruction.

Stakes

Looking again at the original question of the script, there are many ways for Daniel to become a successful oil man. Anderson wants to tell a story about how Daniel achieved his financial and business success. What it cost him. What he looked like as a human before striking oil and what he looks like at the end as a big success: a graying alcoholic sitting on the floor with blood spilled around him and a butler coming downstairs to attend to him.

What does it take for a man to arrive at an ending like that? What would it take, in terms of the events in a character's life, to give him everything and take away everything at the same time? How does this character, during this time in American history, in this industry, in the hands of this writer and director, become a success? That is the question that begins the script. The fact that he succeeds is never really in doubt. What we want to know is *how* – what will it take?

The answer, coming on the heels of the final cycle, is that he must destroy. Anderson creates a story, seen in these three cycles, that shows Daniel destroying as much as humanly possible. Life and livelihoods, the land, and his own dreams of being a father. He must destroy his humanity, too. Put oil in his veins. He succeeds by destroying anything that *isn't* his success. Daniel achieves success as a businessman by obliterating all sense of his own morality, love, and human needs. What's at stake is his humanity, and losing it allows him to make the choices that earn him vast amounts of money.

In the final scene, when Daniel kills Eli with a bowling pin and declares in the last line of the movie, "I'm finished," his journey has come to completion. The audience now has the answer to the initial question posed at the opening of the movie, and this answer is played out with the maximum amount of drama, and yes, in line with the title, blood.

References

Anderson, Paul Thomas (2007) *There Will Be Blood*. Paramount.
DeSica, Vittorio (1948) *Bicycle Thieves*. Ente Nazionale.
Kiarostami, Abbas (1987) *Where is the Friend's House?* Kanoon.
Stanton, Andrew (2008) *Wall-E*. Walt Disney Studios.

The GoFaSt Guide to Screenwriting

9

GOFAST CASE STUDY

Get Out

Get Out

The 2017 Jordan Peele film *Get Out* catapulted to the front of the cinematic world a sub-genre of what has sometimes been called "social thriller" or "social horror." That is, a thriller or horror film that uses genre conventions to demonstrate inequalities – and in the case of this film, racial inequalities – in society. *Get Out* emerged as one of the most acclaimed films of the year with its outrageously inventive and bombastic storyline, clear-eyed casting choices, and visuals that are sparkling in their clarity and symmetry while also being psychologically unsettling.

In the film, photographer Chris Washington, a young black man, is invited by his white girlfriend, Rose Armitage, to meet her family in upstate New York. At the start of the weekend, Rose's parents – Dean, corny and easy-going and presenting himself as racially progressive, and Missy, a more reserved and difficult-to-read therapist – welcome Chris warmly. Chris takes their glad-handing with a cautious goodwill that deteriorates when he notices that the staff are all black and seem to be under some kind of spell. Things become more tense at a party when the sole black guest, who is seemingly under some type of spell, suddenly attacks Chris and begs him to "get out" of this place. As Chris becomes convinced that this place is nefarious and that he should leave an "auction" takes place amongst the white guests as they bid on Chris. The audience learns that the community members have been kidnapping black people, and – with the use of Dean's surgical skills – these aging, frail white people are having their own brains implanted into the bodies of these black men and women. As Chris becomes aware of the scheme, he finds a hidden stash of photographs that show Rose's role in tricking

DOI: 10.4324/9781003141549-9

black men and women to date her and bringing them home, where they will have their brains removed. Chris uncovers this scheme with the help of his best friend Rod Williams, who spends most of the movie coaching Chris by phone, is a proud TSA agent who uses his sleuthing skills to help Chris piece together what is happening. Chris himself is caught and bound and prepped for surgery, but manages to escape in a bloody final confrontation that sees Rose and her family killed and Rod helping Chris leave this upstate town.

Get Out is rich with plotting, and the searing pace keeps the story bouncing along these twists and turns. But the story is not rushed and manages to luxuriate and dramatically embellish the most thematically rich scenes. The ambitiousness of the social commentary, the sheer amount of plot, and the rich character work make this film an intriguing template upon which to examine the GoFaSt model. It's also simply a great film, and therefore highly enjoyable to spend the chapter discussing.

Cycle One

Goal

Get Out introduces protagonist Chris in his Brooklyn apartment, surrounded by framed prints of his black-and-white photographs. He showers and shaves, preparing for a trip, as his girlfriend Rose buys a breakfast of pastries at a bakery. When she arrives at his apartment, Chris is packing, and despite the light mood she's trying to convey, Chris is clearly distracted. She focuses him on a conversation about his feelings, and he reveals that he's worried: she hasn't told her parents that he's black. Rose insists that this is not a problem (she claims that they're progressives and "would have voted for Obama for a third term"), but Chris is not swayed from his concern. He anticipates that, in some way or another, his race will become an issue during this weekend with her family.

Chris's goal, at the beginning of this first cycle, is to have a trouble-free weekend with Rose's family. He wants to avoid awkwardness or tension. Phrased this way, this goal may make him come across as passive, but in fact, he's quite active. During the drive upstate to her parent's house, while Rose is driving, they hit a deer. When the police arrive, they ask for Chris's identification, even though he wasn't driving. Rose confronts the officer for racially profiling Chris, but Chris tries to downplay the event, offering his state-issued identification. Later, at her parents' house, Dean gives Chris a tour of the property and rather forcefully tries to convey to Chris about having no problems with Chris's race – giving the Obama line a try. Chris sidesteps all these matters through rhetorical sidesteps and a calm smile. He is actively trying to avoid any unpleasant, racially charged conversations or engagements and keep the weekend as simple and stress-free as possible.

It is worth noting, too, how the performance by the actor Daniel Kaluuya also mitigates the passiveness that the above descriptions of his character might imply. Casting and performance can inject into the character qualities not written into the action or dialogue of the script. A character who appears cold-hearted and cruel on the page can emerge, in the final, with an air of humanity if the actor can find moments of pause, consideration, or pain to reveal, for instance, in their eyes. The adage "if it's not on the page, it won't be on the screen" is mostly true – but only mostly. And it is important to understand the room that is left to an actor to create nuances in a character between the lines of the script. In *Get Out*, Kaluuya's eyes show "activeness" in what might appear to be passiveness on the page. This happens because each time he de-escalates a tense situation, his eyes show not only a quiet strength that he is choosing to use – and, importantly, letting the offending character that he is choosing to not take strong action – but his eyes also reveal that he is fully cognizant of the social dynamics occurring before his eyes. His gaze shows that he acknowledges with great clarity, for instance, a racist situation with a police officer for what it is, but he's making a choice to let the situation pass without incident – for the sake of his larger goal of a trouble-free weekend.

Failure

About twenty-two minutes into the film, Chris meets Rose's brother, Jeremy, an angry and dangerous young man who seems to have Chris in his crosshairs. A quick cut to that evening's family dinner conversation sees Jeremy further targeting Chris, discussing Chris's potential as a mixed martial arts fighter. Jeremy likens Chris to a "beast," which plays into the running metaphorical language that the film develops, where the racist characters see Chris (and all black people) as animals. Chris continues with his strategy of smiling and rhetorically sidestepping, any potential confrontations, employing emotional restraint to achieve his goal. But when Jeremy, who is drunk, stands up at the dinner table and tries to put Chris into a jiu-jitsu hold, Chris quickly defends himself, and Missy intervenes to stop a potential fight. The physical confrontation fizzles out, but Chris's goal has been undermined. This is no longer a trouble-free weekend. Tension has come front and center in the household, and the awkwardness that Chris has hoped to avoid is now fully on display.

Stakes

Chris is introduced as a confident character who has a strong sense of identity. A talented photographer who has calm, intelligent eyes and an intuitive sense of people, he's a strong protagonist. Given his concerns about the weekend trip, what is at stake for Chris is that he not be exploited, isolated, or otherwise meant to feel "othered" because of his race. This concept winds up being a central theme of the movie (racism as a tool for devaluing certain groups of people), and the stakes for Chris focus on the lens through which the audience will view the movie.

Cycle Two

Goal

The next cycle begins a few hours later when Chris wakes up in the middle of the night. He is distracted by thoughts of the deer that Rose hit and the symbolic resonance this has with his own mother's death after she was hit by a car when Chris was a child. His inability to take action to call for help for his mother, when she failed to come home, has haunted him into adulthood.

Given the threat of physical conflict from Jeremy at dinner (Jeremy's parting line is, speaking about Chris, "I wasn't going to hurt him"), Chris's new goal is to protect himself. With the goal of avoiding awkwardness failed, safety is now his goal as he gets up during the night and goes outside for a smoke.

As we have learned, goals need – among other qualities – to be hard to achieve. If his safety is the goal, the threats must be significant – or, at this early stage in the movie, at least *appear* to be significant. In this second cycle, Chris experiences both real and suggested threats.

The most readily apparent threat is the fact that Chris is vulnerable and outnumbered in the house (being one of the few black people amidst a family of odd and aggressive white people) that is isolated deep in the woods. If another situation like the one with Jeremey arises again, Chris has only himself to rely upon.

Additionally, the film delivers two jump scares that make his goal of safety far from certain. One occurs when Georgina, a creepy-acting maid, suddenly appears in the kitchen, scaring Chris; the other occurs when Walter, an unsettling handyman on the property, comes sprinting at Chris across a yard in the middle of the night. (Both of these workers are black, it should be noted, which Rose's father admits to Chris "looks bad.") When Chris retreats into the house, he is startled by Missy, who uses Chris's smoking habit as a way to put him into hypnosis. During this hypnosis, she renders him paralyzed. Chris enters a "sunken place" where he will now be susceptible, for the remainder of the film, to falling into a hypnotic trance at the sound of a clinking spoon.

Chris's goal of physical safety is challenged again by a highly charged scene where he runs into Walter on the grounds of the estate. Walter is chopping wood with an axe, a prop that looms as a threatening backdrop during an awkward conversation about Rose's attractiveness.

The obstacles to his goal do not end; *Get Out* is relentless in manifesting a wide range of obstacles to Chris's efforts to stay safe. Two scenes after the encounter with Walter, a grand party is hosted at Armitage House. Friends and neighbors attend, all from the nearby community, and all the attendees – except for one curious person – are white. Chris remains an active protagonist, although his actions are subtle. For instance, as a photographer who is frequently taking pictures, he is able to hide behind his camera – or use the excuse of wanting to leave and take some photographs – as an effective strategy for avoiding potential moments of conflict with partygoers (he spends much of the party being ogled and touched in bizarre ways) and therefore asserting his safety.

However, when Chris takes a photograph of the one black attendee, Andrew, this man lunges at Chris in a panic and shouts at him to "get out!" Chris must defend himself against Andrew, another near-miss in a cycle full of threats to his safety.

The totality of these scares and aggressions against Chris is what makes his goal hard to achieve.

Failure

After the incident of Andrew attacking Chris, which Dean attributes to a seizure, Chris and Rose go for a private walk by the lake. But Chris's safety is undermined when – back at the party – Dean is hosting an auction attended by the partygoers. In a startling revelation, what is for sale at the auction is Chris. His attempts for safety are destroyed when he is finally "sold" to Jim Hudson, a blind art gallery owner who wants to use Chris's body for, among other things, sight. Chris has failed at his goal of safety without him even knowing – at least, not yet. The nature and extent of this failure will be revealed to him in the fourth cycle.

Stakes

If the stakes in the first cycle were about Chris's self-worth, and value as a person in the eyes of Rose's family, then the stakes have grown even more dire in the second act. With Chris having been "sold" at an auction, it is his life that is in danger. For the remainder of the movie, Chris will be fighting not just for self-respect but also for his very survival.

Cycle Three

Goal

The third cycle begins quickly, on the heels of the auction. Even though he was not aware that the auction was happening, he gleaned enough threats from the party to know that now he must leave the property. Escaping the Armitage estate is now his third-cycle goal.

This goal is so vital to him (as goals should be in every cycle – of vital significance to the protagonist) that he is planning to leave immediately, with or without Rose. Rose takes this news poorly, at first, but after a conversation about how he feels guilty about his mother's death and he doesn't want to abandon Rose, she agrees to accompany him back to Brooklyn. They'll return to New York together immediately.

This goal fulfills the qualities outlined in Chapter 2, where – among other things – goals are described as needed to be actionable (leaving town certainly is) and verifiable (either he leaves town or doesn't, making his goal something that the audience can clearly see has been achieved or not).

Chris and Rose return to the house as the party is finishing, and Chris heads up to the bedroom to begin packing his bags. However, when Rod calls him with urgency, having figured out that the man who attacked Chris at the party (Andrew) had recently been kidnapped, there is increased urgency to the goal. As she gets her bag, Chris discovers a box with photographs that reveal Rose's role along with her family and community members, in kidnapping scores of black people. This sudden complication makes his goal increasingly difficult to achieve.

Failure

What makes the goal difficult for Chris to achieve – and what causes him to fail – is that he is physically blocked at the door of the house. Jeremy aggressively confronts Chris with a lacrosse stick while Rose holds onto Chris's car keys. A fight ignites between Jeremy and Chris, with Chris trying to push the weapon-wielding man out of the way of the door, and just then, Missy uses the clinking sound of a spoon against a teacup to put Chris into a trance. Thrown out of a conscious state and now vulnerable to whatever the Armitage family wants to do with him, Chris has failed.

It is worth noting that, in the film, Chris states his goal at sixty-two minutes, and his failure occurs at seventy minutes. This is certainly a brief cycle. By comparison, the first cycle took twenty-six minutes, and the second cycle lasted thirty-six minutes. It would probably not come as a surprise that audiences are more attuned to – and care more about – the natural flow of a story's pacing, rather than an artificial and universal standard for how long certain sequences should last on screen. One of the disadvantages of the three-act structure, and other models like it, is that it presumes that all movies – of all genres – will take the same amount of screen time to set up a story, complicate the story, and resolve the story.

The GoFaSt model allows for flexibility for some structural segments to be longer (thirty-six minutes) or shorter (eight minutes), depending on the organic flow of what feels right for the story. What matters is the integrity of each phase being intact (that each goal, failure, and stake should satisfy the qualities described in Chapters 2–4), rather than how many pages a cycle is or how many cycles are written into the script.

In this third cycle, the tight eight pages to run through the three phases – placed in the story at this fast-moving moment – are perfect for bringing the audience through the intensity of Chris going from an outwardly (and falsely, of course) welcome guest at the house to a prisoner.

Stakes

The stakes shift in this cycle, from Chris's safety to his perception of the world. In the first cycle, Chris is established as a canny observer of human nature, attuned to the problems of racial disparities that exist in everyday life. He knows before Rose does (or before she *claims* to know) that there will be racial tensions between her family and him during the weekend. Chris is a character who appears to trust his gut instincts, and the film lets the audience trust him, too. If he thinks something is off, then it's off, and even though the circumstances of the secrets at the Armitage house are hidden from the audience, we believe in Chris to know that we, as the audience, should follow his lead.

However, in this cycle, Rose turns out to be a liar – and Chris had no idea. First, there is the deception he encounters when he finds the box full of pictures featuring her previous lovers. Second, there is a moment when Chris wants to leave the house, and Rose lies that she's trying to find the car keys for him. In fact, she has the car keys – she just refuses to hand them over.

Chris's instincts have failed him. The audience has grown to trust that he can handle difficult situations well – talk or maneuver his way out of problems. But it now appears, in this third cycle, that the grotesque mysterious beings held in the basement of the Armitage house are darker and more awful than even Chris could imagine.

Cycle Four

Goal

The fourth goal in *Get Out* illustrates how goals can sometimes repeat in their type but change in degree. For instance, Chris's goal in the second cycle is to protect himself. There are threats being suggested toward him (and for the most part, they are only suggestions and jump scares), and his guard is up to ensure his safety.

However, in this fourth cycle, the threats against Chris have become greater by many degrees. Chris has been taken into the basement of the house, tied to a chair, and explained (via a video presentation) that his brain is going to be taken from his skull and someone else's brain will be put inside of him. Survival is now his goal. The Armitage family has hurt and kidnapped many people, and presumably, after dispatching with Chris, they will continue to do it many more times. Even though his goal is not explicit in trying to stop the Armitage family's broader plan, by surviving this moment, he may stop future horrors as well. Previously, Chris had been acting toward self-protection; the worst that was happening to him was groping and deranged comments being made to him – which is quite awful, but in this fourth cycle, he's trying to fend off a brain transplant that will turn him – and countless other people after him – into zombified prisoners.

The difficulty of this goal is quite high since he's tied up and under the constant influence of Missy's teacup, which, at any moment, could send him into another trance. The means to achieve this goal must be more extreme, by many orders of magnitude, as well. Whereas in the second cycle, the actions he takes are to parry away from the threats because he is still in the mode of trying to diffuse problems, in the fourth cycle, his actions are supremely (and necessarily) violent. He wields weapons such as a bocce ball and the antlers of a deer head to kill any Armitage family members in his way as he tries to escape. Even Rose dies in the end, as Chris manages to finally achieve his last goal and escape this terrifying town.

Failure

As previously discussed, the final cycle is usually the only cycle where the protagonist has an opportunity to not fail at the goal. If the protagonist succeeds, this is usually a happy ending. If the protagonist fails again, then it is a tragedy.

The ending of *Get Out* shows Chris as victorious, but given the light that the film has shed on the difficult topic of racism, it is clear that the film is not going to deliver a fully happy ending. Chris survives, but there is not much to be happy about in this startling vision of a cruel and unjust world. Therefore, his success at the end is countered with a familiar concept we have discussed where he paid an enormous price for his victory. He has killed people, had a letter opener stabbed through his hand, and been attacked and harmed in many ways. He is wounded and bleeding, a survivor, yes, but one that has been through hell and only barely got out. He does not fail in this final cycle, but there are not many winners, either.

Stakes

The stakes in the final cycle provide a summing up of the central theme of the film. They give a summary thesis of all that we have seen and place it in the context of the world in which we live. At the end of the film, Rod comes to rescue Chris and drive him home. Rod repeats his warning that Chris never should have come to this place. There is a grim pessimism about the state of racism that the film puts forth, its intractability, and the awful outcomes that continue to pain, everyone.

Reference

Peele, Jordan (2017) *Get Out*. Universal Pictures.

The GoFaSt Guide to Screenwriting
10
GOFAST CASE STUDY
Portrait of a Lady on Fire

Portrait of a Lady on Fire

A film of profound depth and feeling, *Portrait of a Lady on Fire* was exceptionally well-received by audiences, critics, and festivals when it premiered in 2019. Among its many award nominations and wins, *Portrait* was awarded Best Screenplay at the 2019 Cannes Film Festival. The film – lusciously shot, brilliantly performed, and exceptionally well-written – is an unabashed arthouse offering, wholly original in its plotline and storytelling rhythms. The script defies specific genre classification and evades easy structural breakdown by most screenwriting models. The subtleness of its plot, weighty emphasis on themes, and heavy leaning toward character-work make for a movie that perhaps feels esoteric; however, there is a great deal of narrative substance beneath its gauzy surface. It is also quite a departure from other films we have analyzed in this book, such as the plot-heavy *There Will Be Blood* or the genre-affirming *Get Out*. Indeed, *Portrait* is a film rich in tone and emotion, and yet breaking down its structure with the GoFaSt model shows a disciplined and efficient narrative that is driving what outwardly appears to be a "loose" and "digressive" storyline.

Let's begin the analysis by walking through the main plot points of the movie:

> In the eighteenth century, a painter named Marianne arrives on a remote island in Brittany with a painting set. She has been commissioned to paint a portrait of Heloise, a young woman from a wealthy family who is about to be married off to a Milanese man – whom Heloise has never met. The painting is to be a gift for the Milanese man in anticipation of

DOI: 10.4324/9781003141549-10

the marriage. Heloise adamantly does not want to get married and, in recent months, refused to have her portrait painted by an earlier painter. Heloise angrily refused to even pose for that painter. Therefore, Heloise's mother, The Countess, has concocted a plan: Marianne will pretend to be a mere companion to Heloise, who – because her sister recently committed suicide – is bereft by loneliness on this isolated island. Marianne will have to study Heloise's face and body features, memorize them, and then paint the portrait in secrecy.

What ensues between the two young women is a friendship that evolves into romance. Themes of art and love, identity and perspective, loom over this masterful film as Marianne and Heloise seek solace and meaning with each other over the course of a fateful few weeks.

The screenplay is rigorously structured and beautifully filmed. The pacing is methodical, which allows for the richness of the actors' performances to linger on screen, creating a feeling of profound authenticity in the emotions they express to each other, and repress in front of The Countess and the maid.

Given the methodical pacing, there are three GoFaSt cycles in *Portrait* – each one is relatively longer than the cycles we examined in the other case studies. Interestingly, the goals that begin each cycle are only subtly different from one another – a curious feature of this script that will be discussed in this chapter. *Portrait* is a film that would be described by many as "character-driven," but as discussed earlier in the book, character-driven films are often – at their core – still plot-driven. The difference in what audiences tend to observe when they make this distinction is *not* that the plot is absent, but rather that the narrative is structured into longer segments that more closely resemble one another than in most so-called "plot-driven" movies.

Cycle One

Goal

Marianne opens the film by teaching a class of painting students. Conveying a wise and quietly wounded demeanor, she turns severe upon noticing that one of the students has taken a painting from a stock room and brought it into the classroom. The painting, which Marianna confesses that she painted, is a stunning image of a woman whose dress is on fire.

The story cuts to the past when Marianne rides a boat through choppy seawaters. She dives into the water to retrieve a blank canvas that has fallen into the waves. The action puts on display Marianne's unique grit and determination as she drags her wet self and soaking canvas onto a beach gnarled by steep hills and brush.

In these opening scenes, the audience knows almost nothing about Marianne in terms of facts or biography – other than the time period during which she lives and that she is a painter and instructor. But a great deal of her personality has come across: warm and intelligent eyes, a strict disciplinarian unafraid of dangers and in control of her surroundings, and haunted by some key events in her past. This is a terrific achievement of writing, directing, and performance to bring the audience so intimately to a character that we know them in an authentic and sophisticated way without yet having been described the facts of their lives. Indeed, portraying facts, information, and backstory on screen can sometimes detract from an audience forming a bond or relationship with a character because the audience becomes burdened with *learning* about who the character is, rather than *feeling* who the character is.

Once Marianne arrives at an estate, she meets Heloise's mother (the Countess) and the maid, Sophie. Both describe Heloise in similar ways: Heloise is a difficult, mercurial woman who recently left the convent and will likely be unkind to Marianne. The audience is also told Marianne's goal: to paint Heloise's portrait. This goal is specific, actionable, and difficult – all requirements that (as described in Chapter 2) satisfy the requirements of a successful goal.

What makes the goal specific? Well, a portrait is a specific object – it either exists or it does not. There is nothing vague or abstract about the existence of a painting.

What makes the goal actionable? Marianne must take several actions to achieve the goal: observe Heloise, memorize her features, and paint alone in secrecy in her studio without being discovered. These actions will take Marianne to various locations and require certain skills (charm, deception, visual memory, and the ability to paint well and quickly) to help make her an active character.

What makes this goal hard to accomplish? Heloise is an oppositional personality: she does not want to marry and therefore would reject having her portrait painted, as this will be a gift for the man she is being forced to marry. A man she has not yet met or even seen. If Heloise will not sit and model for Marianne, then Marianne must paint Heloise from memory by studying her face, and hands, and body during their walks along the ocean shore. Great cinematic technique abounds here, as studying Heloise plays another purpose in that Marianne is slowly falling for Heloise – as is the audience. To truly look at someone and study them creates an opportunity for empathy and connection with that person. Heloise is prickly and keeps Marianne at a distance (and to the audience, she is just as much a mystery as is Marianne), but this close studying of a face and eyes creates an avenue for attachments to build, bonds to develop, and a warmth to develop by truly seeing a person.

Marianne sees much in Heloise that is inspiring and worthy of a stirring portrait. However, painting by mere memory is difficult, and this – combined with having to hide her art supplies and evidence of painting materials in the house so that Heloise does not find them – makes Marianne's goal difficult to achieve.

Failure

The Countess grows impatient with Marianne's slow progress. Marianne herself grows impatient. The painting is not finished. In fact, it is very far from being finished. Days pass, and the portrait is still little more than a sketch with some broad-brush strokes on the canvas. Marianne will fail at the end of this cycle, but the failure must be crisply defined. A potential problem here is that the completion of a painting is not necessarily a hard-and-fast deadline. When does one know that a painting is complete? Any writer or artist will tend to constantly tinker with their work. And a firm deadline has not been attached to her goal. So how does the audience know that Marianne has failed? The failure becomes clear during a conversation between Marianne and Sophie. In a brief exchange, as Sophie serves Marianne a meal, Sophie inquires about the portrait. Marianne expresses frustration with her work. She is not able to capture Heloise's image. As Marianne suggests, a portrait cannot be properly made unless the artist connects with the subject. For instance, Marianne says, she knows so little about Heloise that Marianne has not even seen her smile. Sophie quips that perhaps Marianne should be funny. Marianne grins at the comment and then returns to work on the portrait, where she hesitates with uncertainty at every brush stroke and moves the paint around the rough sketch of Heloise's face – from chin to forehead – without aim or reason. Marianne resigns herself: Sophie was right. Marianne has failed her initial goal of creating a portrait of Heloise because she has not gotten Heloise to smile.

Stakes

Marianne is a painter by trade, having learned the craft from her father, whose name in the art world is highly esteemed. What is at stake is Marianne's professional reputation and, by extension, her father's reputation. She is a dedicated and serious artist who takes the commission seriously; to not paint the portrait or to produce a painting of poor quality, could damage her career and her efforts to take over her father's painting business.

Several scenes in the script emphasize the importance of Marianne's work being a way to sustain her father's esteemed and widely known reputation. The stakes here, as Marianne tries to start her own career from beneath her father's shadow, are not insignificant.

Cycle Two

Goal

Marianne must make Heloise smile. Naturally, the goal is deeper than a mere facial gesture: Marianne must form an emotional connection with Heloise, unravel her mysteries, get this angry and complicated woman to let down her guard, and – ultimately – understand Heloise well enough to be able to paint a faithful portrait of her. It is a clever stroke of dialogue for the character of Sophie to crystalize this important – though vague and unverifiable – goal into a single piece of a specific action. A smile.

This second cycle begins with Marianne meeting Heloise on the beach and having a thoughtful conversation about the suicide of Heloise's sister, their shared experiences of living in convents, and the free will to choose whether they can marry. Heloise is bitter about having little say in the direction that her life takes; Marianne, on the other hand, has the choice to lead her life however she wants. Despite this difference, Marianne believes she is starting to understand Heloise better – and this sentiment carries over into the following scene, where Marianne meets with The Countess and provides some insights into Heloise's emotions.

The following scene shows Marianne making a great deal more progress, quite suddenly, on the portrait. For the first time since she began painting on the island, Marianne appears relaxed and satisfied with her work. Then she dons the green dress that Heloise wears in the painting and sits in front of the canvas. It is an act of empathy and connection to embody another person's clothes and seat, to "stand in their shoes." This act is a continuation of Marianne's growing understanding of Heloise – beyond the mere fascination she had for the woman during the first cycle. As the scene continues, Heloise enters the studio (Marianne must quickly remove the dress and hide the painting set-up), and as the two women smoke a pipe together and talk about music, we see – for the first time in the film – Heloise grin and lightly chuckle during her conversation with Marianne. The warmth that Heloise shows is striking, a significant change from the coldness she had previously been using to arm herself against Marianne.

Failure

Does Heloise's smile count as Marianne's goal succeeding? Close. To begin, as we know, the goal must be difficult to accomplish. Making someone smile may not seem enormously difficult from an outside perspective, so instead of being difficult, this goal is *complicated* (a concept discussed in Chapter 3). As they connect and bond, the women begin falling in love. Marianne hints at feelings of jealousy now that Heloise will be moving to Milan to marry. The smile is not a mere showing of laughter or lightness; rather, it is a sign that the women are falling in love. The angst that accompanies such an impossible romance – given the circumstances of their times and respective situations – makes the relatively "simple" task of making Heloise smile, certainly more complicated than it may initially seem.

Also, the bonding further complicates matters because – given Marianne's romantic feelings for Heloise – Marianne now feels obligated to reveal the truth of her purpose on the island: to secretly paint this portrait. The painting is now finished, and Marianne certainly could have bid Heloise goodbye and left. But honesty is required now, and closure to their brief but meaningful relationship. Marianne decides that she wants to show the portrait to Heloise, and when she does, Heloise dislikes the painting. The portrait is technically impressive but feels generic – it does not capture Heloise's spirit and personality. Heloise states as much, seeing this depiction of her on canvas as a betrayal, and the two women argue.

The failure here comes at a high price to Marianne: she has made Heloise smile, but this has led to a larger failure in the finished painting.

Stakes

If the stakes in the first cycle were related to Marianne's professional ambitions, the stakes in this cycle are deeper: Marianne's emotions. She is falling in love with Heloise and is nervous about being hurt or being discovered for her desires. The commission has turned from professional to deeply personal, and Marianne is now risking more than she initially intended by accepting the job.

Cycle Three

Goal

The last goal of the cycle is a combination of the first two goals: Marianne must paint a new portrait of Heloise – a portrait that, specifically, captures Heloise's spirit. The goal is clearly verifiable because Heloise will apparently be the judge of whether the portrait is correct and meets her expectations.

Each goal of this cycle is a close echo of the other goals. Unlike, for instance, the analysis of *There Will Be Blood*, which shows each goal striking off into new narrative territory ("new" but not random, as each goal is created as an extension of what the previous cycle's failure had set up for the protagonist), *Portrait* feels circular in its narrative construction. The goals are refinements of each other: to paint the portrait, to get Heloise to smile (to make a better portrait), and to paint a new portrait. This structure is not, however, repetitive because each cycle also comes with its unique challenges that make the goal hard to achieve, and each cycle has its own unique failure. The close-quarters of these three goals – like different tenses of the same verb – are part of what makes the movie feel character-driven, even though the plot is clearly (as we're showing in this case study) defined and deliberately structured. Interestingly, for writers seeking this style of art-house fare, where the writer wants to spend a great deal of time and effort on the characters – showing them in many nuances and shades – this version of the model shows a successful way to achieve that.

This third cycle is also notably long – it lasts about fifty minutes. This is a large container to hold the plot and maintain its forward momentum. This can be achieved by maintaining the fundamentals of the cycle. A clear goal – to paint a portrait of Heloise of which she will approve – is made difficult by a series of challenges. Each of these challenges forms a subplot.

First, Sophie reveals herself to be pregnant, and Marianne and Heloise help the maid with her wishes to have an abortion. There are several scenes of the three women preparing Sophie's body for the procedure (having her run across a beach until she collapses in exhaustion, drinking a tea made from wild greens, and hanging by her hands from the ceiling).

Second, the three women drink by candlelight as Heloise reads a passage about the myth of Orpheus trying to help his wife, Eurydice, escape Hades. As the story goes, Orpheus must leave with her without looking back at his spouse. But as they walk, Orpheus cannot contain his enthusiasm to see his wife, turns around, and she is instantly drawn back into the afterlife. The women debate the message of the story, whether desire can be resisted, and how lovers might choose to have the memory of a relationship instead of the relationship itself.

In a third subplot, Heloise and Marianne attend a nighttime bonfire celebration with a group of other women from the island. The celebration feels secretive and ritualistic as the women chant a song in an almost trance-like state. During the scene, Marianne stares with longing and fascination at Heloise from across the bonfire when a lick of flame reaches out and catches the hem of Heloise's dress on fire. Heloise stares boldly at Marianne as Heloise's dress is consumed in flames, which several women douse before Heloise is injured. This image – Heloise on fire – becomes central to Marianne's perception of Heloise as a woman of profound mystery and strength.

How do these subplots manage to feel motivated and escape the problem of becoming episodic? How does the structure hold in such a long cycle? Each of these subplots presents a chapter in Marianne's journey of what it will take to paint a successful portrait: she must get to know herself. The symmetry of this problem is appealing: the first goal fails because she does not know Heloise; the third goal risks failure because Marianne does not yet know herself. Her time with Heloise is, Marianne eventually admits, the first time she has experienced love. She must contend with what the impending affair with Heloise means, and the impossibility that it will last – much like the doomed marriage of Orpheus and Eurydice. The abortion, the myth, and the fire all suggest themes of choice, destiny, creation, and destruction. Heloise mentions that lovers feel like they are inventing something new – like a painting, which Marianne struggles to create. She also participates in creating the romance and ending it too – letting it pass into memory.

Marianne's third cycle begins with her destroying the portrait that Heloise dislikes. In the conversation about the original portrait, Heloise critiques Marianne's belief that a person's spirit, or "presence," as described in the film, is made of fleeting moments that may not be true. Heloise asserts that there is truth in the deepest feelings. Marianne's struggle to complete the goal requires her to find the truth of her own deepest feelings – that is, her love for Heloise – and once she can do that, via the three subplots, then Marianne manages to finish the portrait. Heloise approves, commenting that Marianne would be able to reproduce the image "to infinity." That is: Marianne has found the deeper, permanent truth of her own feelings.

Failure

The final cycle of the movie allows for the goal to be achieved. In *Portrait*, the goal is indeed achieved. How do we know with certainty? There is a shot of Heloise examining the painting as she stands beside Marianne. Marianne states, "finished." The audience naturally pans their glances to watch Heloise, waiting for her verdict. But nothing is said. Instead, the film cuts to a shot of Heloise, undressed and wrapped in bedsheets, smiling at Marianne. This goal pays off, a second time, the second cycle's goal of making Heloise smile – but here, the smile is used for a new purpose: to show Heloise is pleased by what Marianne has painted. The goal has succeeded.

However, the ending is also layered and brilliantly bitter-sweet, because, by completing the painting, Marianne has advanced Heloise's departure for marriage by producing a painting that the suitor – because of Marianne's success – will certainly approve of. Marianne's success is also her failure, as it seals the end of their romance. Marianne's good-bye to Heloise – done in front of the Countess – is painfully brief and chaste, as Marianne turns and hurriedly flees the house to leave the island for good, but not before giving one last look back at Heloise.

Stakes

The bittersweet success of Marianne's goal sets the movie into its final, approximately fifteen minutes of screen time. These last scenes look ahead in Marianne's life, several years after the romance, to show what becomes of her. This is a powerful, deeply moving section of the film, full of melancholy, hope, and loss. There is no specific goal motivating these scenes; rather, it is a sustained elocution of the stakes section of the cycle. It is a summing up of the themes of the film. Here are the important sequences:

First, after the viewing of the painting, Marianne and Heloise are in bed together. Marianne is sketching Heloise's portrait into a locket. Marianne's struggles with producing Heloise's portrait are over; she can now paint her over and over. Marianne's knowledge of Heloise is equal to Marianne's knowledge of herself – an idea that becomes manifest when Marianne sketches a portrait of herself onto the mostly blank page 28 of Heloise's book. The theme of knowledge of self becomes indivisible from the concept of love, that to love is to truly know another, and from this knowledge, the deep truths upon which art is based come to bear. This theme – or stake – is crystalized in this sequence.

The stakes continue to be expressed as the two women lay in bed. Heloise is falling asleep, and Marianne must wake her. The scene that will follow is the cold, painfully polite goodbyes that Marianne bids to Sophie, the Countess, and Heloise, suggesting that even though they have achieved a permanent emotion, art and love are dream-like, and to wake from this dream is to find oneself is the less idealized circumstance of real life. The myth of Orpheus is worked into this thematic reckoning as well, as Marianne urges Heloise to push away any feelings of pain or regret about their romance ending and instead to just "remember." Orpheus had chosen memory over living out a life with his wife – the "poet's choice" – as the women explain earlier in the film. So true, knowing feelings and love are permanent states of a person's soul, but the actual day-to-day life of living with a lover is doomed and will only ever exist as a memory.

The next scenes are shot in cooler hues (as opposed to the warm, candle-lit hues of the bedroom scenes), as Marianne is paid for her work by the Countess, and – under the view of the Countess – Marianne makes her painfully polite final goodbye to Heloise. The Orpheus myth is once again revisited as Marianne is about to exit the mansion when Heloise appears at the stairs, dressed in a white gown similar to the one worn by Eurydice. Heloise asks Marianne to "turn around," and when she does – as happens to Orpheus – Heloise disappears into the darkness.

Years later, Marianne is teaching painting and has come to terms with the relationship: the pain has subsided, and the happy memories have taken their place. Marianne attends an art gallery where one of her paintings – of Orpheus and Eurydice saying goodbye at the moment when she disappears – is on display. Marianne sees another painting at the gallery as well: a portrait of Heloise seated beside her young daughter. In Heloise's lap is a book, and her finger is slipped into the book, opened on page 28. Marianne smiles. One final encounter between the women happens at a concert hall, where Marianne sees Heloise weeping as a symphony plays; Heloise does not see Marianne in the audience, and Marianne does not signal to her. Their relationship remains relegated to the world of memories, to the place where poets live, surrounded by art and memory.

References

Anderson, Paul Thomas (2007) *There Will Be Blood*. Paramount.
Sciamma, Celine (2019) *Portrait of a Lady on Fire*. Pyramide Films.

The GoFaSt Guide to Screenwriting

11

GOFAST CASE STUDY

The Marvelous Mrs. Maisel

Most feature films have a run-time of between 100 and 130 minutes (although in recent years, movies have been getting longer). Episodic television episodes have more flexibility in their length, from "half-hour" shows that usually run in the mid-twenty-minute range to "hour-long" shows that usually run in the fifty-minute range, or even longer than an hour. Even within a given series, there may be a wide range in how long each episode lasts. Run-time becomes less important in the era of streaming, when shows can be paused at any moment and returned later. The length of an episode is dictated less by the requirement for commercial breaks and show scheduling (as was the case during the era of broadcast television) and more by the dictates of the story itself. Pacing and plotting determine how long each episode will run. This increasing variability shows the usefulness of the GoFaSt model, which seeks to structure the natural rhythms of a story and move away from the notion that shows or films – or their structural parts – need to be specific lengths or hit specific page markers.

The Marvelous Mrs. Maisel is a series that premiered in 2017. It tells the story of Miriam "Midge" Maisel, a young woman living in New York City in the 1950s, married to her husband Joel. Together, they have two children. Midge, who lives her days as a housewife taking care of her family, discovers that she has a talent for stand-up comedy and embarks on a journey to liberate herself from the dim expectations of a society that is unwilling to see women as individuals – or funny. *Mrs. Maisel* is a show of extraordinary comedy and wit, managing to develop full and rich characters while masterfully poking fun at the stereotypes that – rampant as they run in society – are not able to constrain the indefatigable spirit of a woman like Midge Maisel.

DOI: 10.4324/9781003141549-11

In this chapter, we will apply the GoFaSt model to the first and third episodes of Season One and observe how the cycles of goals, failures, and stakes work within a shorter-format screen story.

Episode One: Pilot

Cycle One

Goals

The pilot episode runs just over fifty-seven minutes, including credits. After a flashback scene of Midge and Joel's wedding (where Midge shows her talents for standing in front of an audience and telling hilarious stories), the story turns to Joel working in sales at a plastics company. Spending his days wearing a dull gray suit and working in a midtown Manhattan office, worried that he's doing little more with his life than pushing around stacks of papers and attending boring meetings, Joel dreams of downtown life. In this fantasy, he wears bohemian black turtlenecks and performs stand-up comedy in front of hip Manhattan crowds roaring with laughter at his jokes. Midge, ever doting on Joel, supports him by preparing his precious turtleneck while taking care of the kids, as well as looking after her parents, who live in the same apartment building as Midge and Joel.

This first GoFaSt cycle naturally begins with a goal for our protagonist, Midge. As we know, goals should be specific and actionable, and while Midge's broader goal is to support Joel in his dreams, specifically, her goal is to use her charms (and baking abilities) to get Joel a good slot at the evening open mic events at his favorite comedy club, The Gaslight. "Being supportive" is an attribute or characteristic of Midge, but it is not an actual goal in a dramatic sense. A goal should be more specific and allow for a definable ending, where the goal has either been achieved or not, in a pragmatic way. The show creates this type of goal as Midge bribes and cajoles the manager of the club, Baz, to get Joel these prized times (not too early in the evening when crowds haven't arrived and not too late when everyone begins to leave).

Midge is content with this goal: she loves Joel and finds his stand-up act to be quite clever. During his comedy set, she diligently takes notes in a pink notebook and gauges the audience's reactions to each punchline to provide him with useful feedback to help him improve.

The one obstacle that Midge runs into is a surly bartender named Susie. Susie knows quality comedy, and she finds Joel's act to be less-than-funny. Susie also resents Midge's constant sunny disposition and her thinly veiled manipulations of the club manager.

The notion of Midge "being supportive" – though not a goal – is nevertheless vital information. It motivates her other, smaller actions and goals. One such goal is her desire to prop up Joel's ego by making him think he is going to sleep every night with a wife who is something of a beauty queen. (Part of Midge's eventual growth is to stop accommodating Joel's fragile ego and immature view of the world.) This sequence occurs during Midge's nightly routine of going to sleep with make-up on and her hair perfectly done to provide Joel with a picturesque view of his stunning wife. After he falls asleep, she hustles to the bathroom to remove her makeup, apply cold cream all over her face, and put curlers in her hair. The following mornings, she wakes before Joel and reapplies her makeup and restyles her hair, so that when he wakes up, he sees only this vision of perfection.

Goals can – and usually do – spring from a character's attitude or general belief system, but attitudes and beliefs themselves are not goals, and the notions should be used interchangeably. Belief systems give rise to goals but are not necessarily actionable in-and-of themselves.

Failure

Twenty-two minutes into the pilot, Midge sees on television the famous comedian Bob Newhart performing a comedy act on the Ed Sullivan Show. Midge hears Newhart doing the same act that Joel performs at the Gaslight. Alarmed, she tells Joel that Bob Newhart stole his act. Joel confesses that he, in fact, stole the act from Newhart. Midge is appalled as Joel admits that most comedians steal each other's acts, especially when they're just starting out – like Joel. Midge is confused and disappointed by Joel's confession, but takes his insights to be true.

The failure here is not Midge's, but Joel's. She admits to being naïve, expressing that she's new to the goings-on and protocols of comedy; however, Joel's characterization of comedy as an art form where stealing is allowed, even expected, is not true. Her naivete is in believing so blindly in her husband (a man who is not sturdy and wise enough to be entrusted with such faith), whom she had assumed had written those wonderful stand-up jokes himself.

The failure is that even though Midge gave Joel everything he needed to help him succeed on stage (the chosen time slot, the turtleneck, etc.), his success is worthless. The laughs are a fraud. His jokes are stolen. She propped him up, but her efforts were for naught.

This version of failure is cleverly staged and creates enormous sympathy for Midge from the audience. Her support of Joel is unfailing, and her smarts and charms seem unable to ever be stopped. At this point in the story, the audience doesn't necessarily want to see Midge fail: she's the smart one in the relationship, the strong one, and actually the funny one. The protagonist needs to fail, structurally speaking, but in this case, the audience needs to see how talented she is. So it is Joel who fails her, which not only boosts her capabilities in the eyes of the audience but also casts Joel in a dim light, making him into an emerging antagonist of the story.

Stakes

Joel's comedy is so closely tied to his happiness that anything undermining his comedy risks making him unhappy. Midge's every action is meant to make Joel a happy husband; this motivation is partly created by her true and actual love for him, but also partly created by society's expectations of her (in 1950s America) that a wife's primary duty is to serve her husband.

Until this confession about the stolen comedy material, all had seemed well in the Maisel household. From the opening wedding scene that was full of laughs and love between Midge and Joel to their adventures in the downtown comedy scene, happiness is in no short supply for this family. But with this failure creating the first fault line in their family, what's at stake is the happiness of Midge and Joel's relationship.

Cycle Two

Goal

Joel has another comedy set lined up, and this time he's a nervous wreck because his and Midge's close friends – Archie and Imogene – will be attending. After some snafus that ramp up his nerves (they are late getting to the comedy club, and his sweater has holes in it), Midge once again has a goal: to help Joel succeed on stage by getting him the best time slot. The repetition of her goal is indicative of her life as a 1950s American housewife, which is itself a repetitive cycle of caring for her children all day and then caring – with as much pandering and handholding – for her husband in the evenings.

However, goals should not exactly repeat themselves from one cycle to the next for obvious reasons of becoming stale, and so in this cycle, she has a twist on how to help Joel: she suggests that he'd do well on stage to talk about the holes in the turtleneck. By talking about this, she hopes he might be more personal on stage, more authentic, and deliver some jokes that are truly his own. Midge's goal is once again to help Joel succeed on stage, but this time, her goal is to manifest his success by helping him tap his inner talents.

Failure

Unfortunately, Joel has no inner talents. When he attempts to be more personal and joke about his sweater, his jokes are terrible. Joel becomes awkward on stage; everyone in the audience grows bored and awkward. To salvage the performance, he attempts to revert to his stolen jokes, but he's become so flustered that he can't perform them well. His evening on stage is a disaster.

This is certainly a failure, and once again, it is Joel's failure – not Midge's. She delivered hilarious jokes about his turtleneck on the cab ride to the comedy club, jokes that he's not able to replicate or build upon. This shows that she was right – being personal and original could have worked for him on stage if only he had any of her comedic talents. Joel fails Midge, but because they are a team, this failure rests on her shoulders as well.

The failure continues when they arrive home, and Joel decides that he's so humiliated and frustrated that he must leave Midge. He packs his suitcase (which ends up being her suitcase, in fact, since he's unable to do anything right), and he leaves her. He walks out of the marriage, also admitting that he's having an affair with his secretary.

Stakes

Joel's frustrations as a comedian have reached a tipping point, and instead of coming to the realization that comedy isn't for him (and suspecting that she's the true comedian of the family), he blames her for his failures. Their marriage is destroyed, and the stakes now are enormous: rather than the couple's happiness being at stake, their very marriage – and Midge's domestic future – now risks being lost.

Cycle Three

Goals

The second cycle of the pilot episode is just over ten minutes long. Rather short but powerful, it contains the three ingredients of the cycle and pushes the story briskly into the third and final cycle of the episode.

The third cycle begins with Midge telling her parents that Joel has left her. She has no choice, and time is of the essence: tomorrow is Yom Kippur, and she is inviting many guests to the observance dinner, including her parents and the rabbi, whom everyone hopes to impress. Midge's parents are devastated by the news, and her father gives Midge very stern advice: put on a pretty dress, reapply make-up, and go find Joel to bring him home. Midge does not necessarily want Joel back, but she sees the necessity of trying to return to the normal operations of her life. The kids need a father. Midge needs financial support. And the dinner must go off smoothly.

At home, Midge sees that her Pyrex is missing. In fact, the dish is at the comedy club (she had brought it to the club with a brisket to compel the owner to give Joel a favorable time slot in the first cycle). Because she needs the Pyrex to cook for Yom Kippur, Midge returns to the comedy club. This is her goal: get the Pyrex so that the dinner can happen and her life can return to normal. Drunk now, unruly, and angry, she ascends the club stage while waiting for the return of her Pyrex, and launches into an impromptu comedy routine. Her jokes – personal and relating to Joel's abandonment – are fantastic. The crowd loves her act. Midge is so drunk and compelled to tell her story that she reveals her breasts to the crowd and is promptly arrested and sent to jail.

Failure

The failure is that Midge does not get her Pyrex (and the chance for a normal, happy family dinner). Instead, she spends the evening getting bailed out, nursing a hangover, wearing someone else's shoes (she doesn't know how this happened), and listening to the surly bartender Susie tell Midge that she could have a career in comedy.

Stakes

The stakes in the final cycle of a show or film usually encapsulate the theme of the protagonist's journey. At the end of Midge's failure, Susie makes the proposition that Midge should pursue a career in comedy, and Midge can help. Susie even puts forth her own belief that she wants to help because she was something significant in her life. Helping Midge capitalize on her talent would be significant. This is a useful conversation for two reasons. First, it provides a worldview and motivation to Susie that she might be able to take on some of the protagonist roles in the upcoming episodes. Second, it spells out what this episode has been about living a life of significance. Susie may be speaking about her own life, but it also applies to Midge's. Her life with Joel was a background player to his weak starring role; her life had no significance outside the walls of her house. But going on this journey (these three cycles), Midge has discovered that she can lead a life of significance, and this sets up for the second episode, where she will take the first step in achieving that.

Episode Three: Because You Left

This analysis looks at the third episode of Season One of *The Marvelous Mrs. Maisel*. Episode two largely follows the various characters reeling from the news of Midge and Joel's breakup. The episode introduces the audience to Joel's father (Moishe) and explores his relationship with Midge's father (Abe) and the tension between the two men, as well as Midge's mother using a fortune teller to help ease the anxiety over the divorce. At the end of the second episode, Moishe throws Midge out of the apartment where she lives, and Midge performs a stand-up comedy routine that, because of her use of curse words in a public setting (which breaks the decency codes of the time), lands her once again in jail.

Here are the cycles of episode three:

Cycle One

Goals

Following a brief flashback that shows Joel and Midge meeting in college, the episode opens with Midge in jail. She is bailed out by the famed comedian Lenny Bruce (whom she had met when he was also being jailed at the same time), and Lenny informs Midge that because of her arrest, she will have to retain a lawyer. Midge confers with Susie, and as a court date looms for Midge to defend herself against the charges, Midge and Susie meet with a lawyer.

Midge's goal is to fight the charges against her. As her lawyer states, the charges against her are an infringement on her freedom of speech, and Midge – especially in her pursuit of honest comedy – cares deeply that such freedom remains intact. Midge's goal is full legal exoneration.

Failures

In court, Midge and her lawyer face a judge who is openly chauvinistic. He belittles Midge, treats her like a child, and insists that she needs her husband by her side to deal with this court hearing. Midge does not respond well at all, and despite her lawyer making headway in getting the charges dismissed (in exchange for Midge promising to never speak with foul language again), Midge stands up against the judge and forcefully (and with plenty of cursing) refuses to agree to anything the judge wants from her. Consequently, Midge is thrown into jail.

The failure here is clear: Midge wanted to be found innocent of the charges against her, but instead winds up creating a scandal in court and getting jailed for the third time in nearly as many days.

Stakes

Midge is not scared of being in jail. Her safety or well-being is not at stake. Midge is a character who is strong, smart, and capable of taking care of herself. None of those things could reasonably be at stake at this moment in the narrative. What is at stake, though, is babysitting care for her kids. Currently, her two small children are at her parents' house, being cared for with the help of a nanny. But Midge's overly dramatic mother and constantly angry father mean that the children should not stay very long – Midge needs to be back with them soon. Their well-being is what is at stake.

Cycle Two

Goals

Episodic television has, in general, more plot lines than most feature films. The goals are sometimes introduced in a previous cycle, and the failures get paid off in a later cycle. We saw this in the analysis of *There Will Be Blood*. There can also be more variety of characters who introduce a goal and experience the failures. It is not only the central protagonist who carries this narrative responsibility; supporting characters can also do this – supporting characters who sometimes take on the protagonist's narrative responsibilities. In this way, the GoFaSt model applies to stories with a single protagonist or an ensemble cast. If the cycle features a character about whom the audience cares and who carries significance in the plot, there can be flexibility as to whose goal is the focus of the cycle.

This is especially true, as stated above, on television. In *Ms. Maisel*, there are three characters who establish a goal in the second cycle. The goals all begin around the same time and turn into failures around the same time, too.

The first goal is Abe's. He is trying to get Joel and Midge back together. His reason for this is simplicity – everyone's lives will go much more smoothly and make more sense if the marriage remains intact. A traditionalist, Abe sees no good outcome to the divorce. To achieve this goal, he goes to Moishe – a sometimes nemesis – and proposes a strategy for getting their kids back together: instead of Moishe selling the apartment where Joel and Midge lived, Abe suggests that he buys half the apartment from Moishe and they own it together, keeping it as a stable place where Joel and Midge can return as a family.

The second goal is shared by Susie and Midge and occurs during a conversation after Midge is released from prison. Midge feels that she cannot live without comedy – she needs not only the monetary compensation that the work would provide (as a divorced woman who had only been a homemaker while married, she now needs an income), but she also needs to feel the passion of the craft. She loves comedy and can't imagine living without it. Midge explains that she has no choice but to be a success. This is her goal. What does a successful goal look like? Being on stage and getting to perform regularly.

Susie also states a goal here: she promises to help turn Midge into a big success. Susie guarantees this. What does success look like to Susie? The same as it looks to Midge, with Midge performing on stage to roaring audiences on a regular basis.

All three characters have actionable and specific goals, and the rest of the cycle sees their failures emerging to varying degrees.

Failures

Abe's failure comes at the end of the episode. After a long day in jail and hanging out at the club, Midge returns home to find Joel standing outside the building. Joel does not look well – he's stressed and exhausted, and his affair, which may have seemed so exciting at first, he now finds annoying and frustrating. Joel asks for Midge to be back; he wants to be married to her again. The scene cuts to Midge walking into her apartment and telling her father that she saw Joel, and she relates Joel's request. Abe becomes hopeful. But Midge explains to Abe that she refused Joel. She will not go back to him because, she says simply, he left her. Abe's goal of reuniting his daughter and her husband has – at this point in the story, at least – failed. What does this mean for Abe? He will either have to give up and change as a person, or he will have to try again using a different tactic. Either way, he is set up for an interesting new goal in the next cycle.

Susie and Midge's failures are not quite as fatal. Susie's goal – where she promises Midge success – meets reality when Susie goes to the members-only Friars Club to meet with a successful talent manager whom she knows. Because she is not a member (and not, therefore, "significant" as she said in the first episode), she is nearly thrown out but eventually allowed to stay. The manager deems Susie to be rude and difficult, but he also admires her pluck and drive. Susie must admit to him her predicament: she wants to manage a comedian but has no idea how to be a manager. The mentor promises to help her at a later date and leaves. Susie's failure is not a complete one, it merely is a setback: she is too inexperienced to achieve her goal, and the information she needs to succeed will be delayed.

Finally, Midge's failure is – like Susie's – more of a stutter step, or pushback, than a complete failure. When Midge meets up with Lenny Bruce and some of his musician friends, she gets high and decides to introduce the band at the club where they're playing. But her introduction is a mixture of funny jokes and bizarre behavior (she's high on pot at the time) and winds up as a kind of mess when she forgets to even introduce the band. Even Lenny isn't sure what to make of Midge. If Midge's goal is success, she is showing herself to still be a very raw talent – more raw than talent, even – whose impulsivity and inexperience show her chances of success to be slim indeed.

Failures are not meant to end a story, naturally, only to push the protagonist in a different direction to try success from a different angle. Each of these failures does not end anyone's efforts, rather, the failures show that every character's initial assumption about what it will take to succeed is wrong, and new paths – and more growth – will be required to eventually achieve these goals.

Stakes

The stakes in these three failures are remarkably similar. What is at stake for Abe, Susie, and Midge is that they all have images in their heads of what they want life to look like. What is at stake, and what is the theme at the end of this episode, is this notion of having dreams and what it is like to see those dreams, if not dashed, then delayed. The next episodes, and subsequent cycles will continue working on these dreams and goals until – eventually – they become attainable for each character.

Reference

Sherman-Palladino, Amy (2017) *The Marvelous Mrs. Maisel*. Amazon Studios.

The GoFaSt Guide to Screenwriting

12
CONCLUSION

At this conclusion of the book, it is useful to step back and ask about the larger purpose of developing new screenwriting models. Great movies have been written on the existing models, so why do we need anything new? The old but often-correct adage, "If it ain't broke, don't fix it," comes to mind. And there is certainly nothing broken about the Aristotelian three-act structure. Other canonical texts on screenwriting, such as Christopher Vogler's *The Writer's Journey*, and the foundational books upon which they are derived, like Joseph Campbell's *Hero with a Thousand Faces*, are definitely not broken. The models laid out by these masters and masterworks have led to the creation of much greatness in cinema.

Why do anything differently now?

One part of answering this question lies in the observation that these existing models will, of course, endure. It is implausible to think that they should ever be replaced. Inventing new models of screenwriting does not imply doing away with existing models – rather, a screenwriter would benefit by using several models at once. Or, at least, keeping several models close at hand. When one does not seem to be solving the screenwriter's problem of telling a story, one can move over to a different model and look for inspiration there. The more access that a writer has to new modes of thinking and new perspectives from which to improve their work, the better.

Innovation has allowed cinema to evolve over time. When synchronized sound was invented, the requisite audio-recording and sound amplification inventions didn't come about because there was an existing problem in the film. The silent era of filmmaking is one of the grandest and most creative eras ever to exist in the history of cinema. There was nothing "broken" about the films of Charlie Chaplin, Sergei Eisenstein, Carl Theodore Dreyer, or the early films of Alfred Hitchcock. But the synchronized sound was invented because innovation – on its own terms – is unstoppable, and so new kinds of films emerged.

The same is true of technical inventions in the speeds of film stocks and lighter film cameras that allowed novice filmmakers in France in the 1950s to pick up cameras on their own – without the backing of large crews and big budgets – and change the world by creating the French New Wave. The digital filmmaking era and the invention of DSLR cameras have created many opportunities for hobbyists or aspiring filmmakers to step into the art form and produce great works. These innovations lower the cost of entry to make a film and invite more voices to the table, and cinema benefits from this. Innovation doesn't come at the expense of earlier models, and its arrival doesn't imply that anything prior was "broken." It comes of its own volition to the benefit of filmmakers and audiences alike.

A new screenwriting model, like a new type of lighting equipment that is lighter and consumes less energy, is merely another tool in the toolbox of filmmaking. When the filmmaker Steven Soderbergh announced his retirement from feature filmmaking (before unretiring some months later), he talked about having mastered the tools in the filmmaker's toolbox. His articulation of this matter suggested a sort of boredom with those tools – he'd used them all and grown a bit weary.

The same can be true of screenwriters relying upon the traditional models of screenwriting. A writer struggling in the middle of the second act can turn to an existing model for instruction – a refresher or reminder – about how to successfully get through this difficult section of a script. There is some security in knowing that this model has worked, in the past for so many.

But it's also possible to feel, if not bored by these often-used solutions, at least somewhat uninspired. People get into mental ruts the more they do a certain task; we get used to doing something the way that we have always done it and are therefore increasingly likely to do it in the same way in the future. Habits form quickly and become deeply engrained in our minds – and in our creative endeavors. It is certainly possible that by looking in the same *place* for answers over and over, the writer will keep coming up with the same answer. This is not necessarily healthy for the creative mind. Does the three-act model lead screenwriters to find solutions and ideas that are mere versions of the same ideas they've previously had? It would be unfair to answer an unequivocal yes since this model is robust enough to serve as a platform for a great variety of stories. But the answer might be a partial yes. The screenwriter wants to be excited – wants to learn something new, expand their language, reach for new ideas, and look in undiscovered places – for writing solutions to help them push and make them better.

In some ways, the GoFaSt model is a new way to look at old ideas. In other ways, it is new on its own terms. Regardless, screenwriters are innovating and pushing the formal boundaries of screen storytelling. New platforms for watching films and television mean that run times are changing, the way that audiences watch these stories is changing, and expectations for how these new stories will make us feel or think are changing. Innovative screenwriting and television writing are all around us.

Just one wonderful example is the feature film *Ma* written and directed by Celia Rowlson-Hall. It is a road movie about a couple traveling across the desert. There is no dialogue in the movie. It is not a silent movie – there are plenty of diegetic sounds. Rather, it's just that no one seems to talk in the film. It is an extraordinary and novel film. If writers and filmmakers are pushing the boundaries of this hundred-year-old art form forward in such expansive and explosively creative ways, new models will be helpful along the way to help inspire new solutions to old screenwriting problems.

The GoFaSt model seeks a more organic, free-flowing way to write a script – to bring structure (but not formula and not heavy-handed rules or rituals) to screenwriting. It seeks to appeal to new screenwriters who are reticent to accept the old ways of doing something, as well as more seasoned writers searching for tools and ideas they had never previously considered. This model seeks to be an aide to comfort in writing and innovation and to provide the fresh perspective for which all artists yearn.

References

Campbell, Joseph (1949) *The Hero with a Thousand Faces*. Pantheon Books.
Vogler, Christopher (2007) *The Writer's Journey: Mythic Structure for Writers*. Michael Wiese Productions.

INDEX

1917 (film) 20, 42

actionable goal 14–15, 16, 48, 59, 83, 96, 102, 110
actionable journey 31
action film 9
action sequence 67
alienating the audience 43
Alien franchise 47
aliens in film 59
ambiguity 9, 15, 82
Anderson, Paul Thomas *see There Will Be Blood*
animal attack 25
animals as plot drivers 38, 62; *see also* dog as plot point
Aristotle 3, 12, 119; *see also* three-act structure
art-house style 105
Aster, Ari: *Hereditary* 47–48; *Midsommar* 46, 47–48
avant garde 43
Avildsen, John G.: *Rocky* 21, 31, 43

Babadook, The 47–48
Baby Driver 69
backstory 50, 53, 60, 62, 65, 66, 81, 102
bad guys 69
Being John Malkovich 5
Bicycle Thieves 17, 38, 84
big-budget film 9, 67, 120
Bigfoot 18–19

Birds of Prey 58
Blade Runner 15
blockbusters 73
Blair Witch Project 47
boredom 7, 112, 120
Borzage, Frank: *7th Heaven* 57
budgets 12; big-budget 9, 67, 120; limitation of 1, 11; low-or-moderate budget 47–48; marketing 57

Cabinet of Dr. Caligari 52
Campbell, Joseph 119
Caron, Glenn Gordon: *Clean and Sober* 21
Carpenter, John: *Escape from New York* 20
Cassavetes, John: *A Woman under the Influence* 5, 30
Cast Away 30
Chaplin, Charlie 57, 119
character arcs 4, 10, 13, 17
character development 1, 51, 109
character-driven film 14, 25, 37, 101, 105
character motivation 9, 19, 31, 41, 58, 83, 86
Chariots of Fire 43
Clean and Sober 21
Coen, Joel and Ethan 8, 28, 74, 79; *No Country for Old Men* 19, 29; *Raising Arizona* 29

comedy 21, 28; horror-comedy 47; *Raising Arizona* 29; romantic 25, 36; stand-up, representation of (*Maisel*) 109–117
complexity in a script 20
confusion in a script 20
Coppola, Francis Ford: *Godfather, The* 42, 69, 70
Cruise, Tom 9

Danish Girl 43
D.C. superhero films 67
death as means of establishing or raising stakes 37–38, 42; *Babadook* 48–51, 53; *Get Out* 94, 96; superhero movie example 63–64, 66
deception 97, 102
DeSica, Vittorio: *Bicycle Thieves* 17, 38, 84
desperation of character 8, 70, 71, 74, 80
destination (getting to), as type of goal 21, 64
destiny 43, 106
didacticism, avoiding 14, 40
difference, allowing to occur 5, 13, 26, 44, 101
difficulty of goal, for character 17
Dog Day Afternoon 18, 29–30, 38
dog as plot point 28–29
Dreyer, Carl Theodore 119; *The Passion of Joan of Arc* 43; *Vampyr* 52
DSLR camera 120
dumbing down 14

Ebert, Roger 24
Eisenstein, Sergei 119
empathy, as created by films 24, 25, 26, 32
empathy, as experienced by characters 102, 104
Escape from New York 20
Eternal Sunshine of the Spotless Mind 16

failures, as experienced by characters 8, 13, 20, 24–33; as catalyst for change 28; characters developed through 25–27; characters' weakness exposed by 25; complicating 29; concept of 22; as equalizer 26; lessons learned via 32; loss of important possession 31; nature of 24–26; new story element of 30; outsmarted 31–32; physically stopped 30; self-destruction 31; Sonny (*Dog Day Afternoon*) 18; resonant 28; qualities of 28–30; study guide 33–34; types of 30–32; unexpected 28–29; varieties of 26
Farhadi, Asghar 79
fear, as primal human emotion 25–26
fears of audience, using films to experience or confront 24, 29, 46; *Blair Witch* as example of 47
fears of character 33, 41, 51, 62, 63
feelings of audience 16, 24; empathy for character 32, 102; manipulating 28; using music to impact 36
feelings of character 9, 26, 67, 71; internal thoughts and 37; romantic 104, 107–108
Ferris Bueller's Day Off 33
Figgis, Mike: *Leaving Las Vegas* 31
"fill in the blanks" approach to outlining 50, 66, 78
Fitzgerald, F. Scott 81
Ford, John 79
four-act structure 3
Frankenstein; Or, The Modern Prometheus 13–14
free from morals 17–18
French New Wave 120
Friedkin, William 79
From Dusk to Dawn 47

Get Out: GoFaSt exercise 91–99
goals 11–23; actionable 14–15, 16, 48, 59, 83, 96, 102, 110; authentic 18; complicating 29; destination (getting to), as type of goal 21, 64; difficulty of, importance of 17; failure at achieving 26, 32, 34, 37, 40; *Ferris Bueller* 33; five types of 19; *Get Out* 92, 94–95, 98–99; heist film exercise 70, 73–74, 75–76; horror exercise 48–49, 53–54, 55; *Marvelous Mrs. Maisel* 110–111, 112–113, 113–114, 115, 116–117; money as 43; moral 17; non-morality in 18; personal redemption, as type of goal 20, 21; physical object as type of goal 19–20;

Portrait 101–102, 105–106; qualities of 14–18; resonant failures leading to changing of 28; saving someone, as type of goal 20; self-destructiveness thwarting achievement of 31; short term 42; simple, linear, and straightforward 41, 72; stakes, in relationship to 35; study guide 22–23; superhero exercise 58–60, 61–63, 65–66; *There Will Be Blood* 83, 86–87; types 18–22; verifiable 15–16, 59, 62–4, 96, 105; unverifiable 104
goals, failures, stakes (GoFaSt): basic structural machinery driving characters' narrative journey 13; cycle of 8, 56, 110; establishing 47; *see also* goals; failures; stakes
Godfather, The 42, 69, 70
GoFaSt Model 1–10; metaphor to visualize 8–9; what happens next 8
Gondry, Michael: *Eternal Sunshine of the Spotless Mind* 16
Good Time 14, 16

Hamlet 13, 14
happiness 15–16, 25, 32, 112–113
Haynes, Todd: *Joker* 58
Heart of Glass 52
Heat 69
heist film 15; *Dog Day Afternoon* 29; GoFaSt exercise 69–77
Hellboy 47
Hereditary 47–48
hero's journey 3, 7
Herzog, Werner: *Heart of Glass* 52
Hitchcock, Alfred 120
Hollywood: actioners 9; earliest films of 57; marketplace 76; thriller 36, 38; writing 43
Homer: *Odyssey* 13
Hooper, Tom: *The Danish Girl* 43
Hoosiers 81
horror genre: GoFaSt exercise 46–56; low-budget 47; *see also Get Out*
horror-sci-fi 47
horror-superhero 47
Hudson, Hugh: *Chariots of Fire* 43
Hughes, John: *Ferris Bueller's Day Off* 33; *Planes, Trains and Automobiles* 21

Huston, John: *Maltese Falcon, The* 42; *Treasure of the Sierra Madre, The* 19
hyper-directionality 29
hypnotism 52, 94

Jack Reacher 9
Joker 58
Jonze, Spike: *Being John Malkovich* 5

Kaluuya, Daniel 93
Keaton, Buster 57
Keaton, Michael 21
Kent, Jennifer: *Babadook, The* 47–48
Kiarostami, Abbas: *Where is the Friend's House?* 17, 84
killer, identifying the 81
Killing, The 42
Knives Out 31, 81
Kubrick, Stanley: *The Killing* 42; *The Shining* 30

Lean, David 79
Leaving Las Vegas 31
linearity, in storytelling 7–8, 20–1, 37, 41, 88
logline 2
loneliness of character 58, 89, 101
loss: of fight (*Rocky*) 43; of important possession (*Pulp Fiction*) 31; of life (*Good Time*) 15; of motivation 31; romantic (*Portrait of Woman on Fire*) 107
low-budget film: horror 47
Lumet, Sidney: *Dog Day Afternoon* 18, 29–30, 38
Lynch, David: *Mulholland Drive* 5

Ma 121
Mad Max 65
Maltese Falcon, The 42
Mann, Michael: *Heat* 69
Marshall, Neil: *Hereditary* 47–48
Martin, Steve 21
Marvelous Mrs. Maisel 75; GoFaSt case study 109–118
Marvel superhero films 67
McQuarrie, Christopher 9, 21; *Jack Reacher* 9
Mendes, Sam: *1917* 20, 42
mental illness 31, 58
Midsommar 46, 47–48
Milius, John: *Red Dawn* 42

Miller, George: *Mad Max* 65
Mission Impossible series 9
monster 13; *see also* Bigfoot
moral framework 81
moral bankruptcy 70
morality 41, 90
morals 17–18, 28; immoral 40
motivation *see* character motivation
Mulholland Drive 5
murder as means to establish or raise stakes 64, 87
murder mystery 81
Murnau, F. W.: *Nosferatu* 46
Myrick, Daniel, and Sanchez, Eduardo: *Blair Witch Project* 47

No Country for Old Men 19, 29
Nosferatu 46

Ocean's Eleven 69
Odyssey, The 13
Orpheus myth 106, 108
outsmarted, as type of failure 31–32

pacing of story 6, 13, 38, 78, 82–83; controlling 88; *Get Out* 96; plot and 22, 109; *Portrait of a Lady on Fire* 101; *There Will Be Blood* 88–89
Passion of Joan of Arc 43
Peele, Jordan 91; *Get Out* GoFaSt exercise 91–99
personal redemption, as type of goal 20, 21; Rocky Balboa 43
physical object as type of goal 19–20
Planes, Trains and Automobiles 21
plot: character-driven movies' need for 37; character failure in relationship to development of 25; *Get Out* 92; goals in relationship to 55; instigating 60; McQuarry on 9; over-plotting 30; pacing and 22, 109; *Portrait of a Lady on Fire* 100–101, 105–106; as skeleton 10; too fast 88; *see also* story; subplot
plot circumstance 16
plot direction 53, 58
plot-driven stories 14, 25, 101
plot elements 63, 65, 75
plotlines 61; in episodic television 116
plot mechanics 9, 10, 13, 22
plot summary 2

plot vs. story 10, 21
Portrait of a Lady on Fire 22, 75; GoFaSt case study 100–108
preachiness, avoiding 14, 40
predictability 4, 34, 55; too predictable, plot as being 44; unpredictability 33
predicament 75, 117
pregnancy 106
Pulp Fiction 19, 21, 31, 33, 42

racism in film 93, 98, 99; *see also Get Out*
Raising Arizona 29
Red Dawn 42
redemption *see* personal redemption, as type of goal
Reichardt, Kelly 79; *Wendy and Lucy* 28
rejection: of film 44; of script 3; of scriptwriting models 5
roadblocks 48, 50
Rocky 21, 31, 43
Rodriguez, Robert: *From Dusk Till Dawn* 47
romance 57, 60; end of 107, 108; friendship evolving into 101, 104, 106
romantic comedy 25, 36
romantic relationship 38, 104
Rowlson-Hall, Celia: *Ma* 121
run-time 109

Safdie, Josh and Benny: *Good Time* 14, 16; *Uncut Gems* 41
"save the cat" plot structure concept 69, 78
saving someone, as type of goal 20
science fiction genre (sci-fi) 62; horror-sci-fi 47
Scorsese, Martin: *Taxi Driver* 43
Scott, Ridley: *Blade Runner* 15
screenplay: as bedrock of filmmaking 1; Best Screenplay Award (Cannes) 100; developing 12; diagramming protagonist's failures in 34; as distinct from novel 9; hypothetical screenplay based on concept of screenplay being stolen 70–77; ideas for 11; failure as crucial to plot of 28, 33; need for something to go wrong in plot of 27; plot as beats of 9–10; stakes, importance in plot of 37; structure 78; writing and rewriting/revising 22, 34

126 Index

self-destruction, as type of failure 31
Seventh Heaven 57
Shakespeare, William: *Hamlet* 13, 14
Shaun of the Dead 47
Shelley, Mary: *Frankenstein; Or, The Modern Prometheus* 13–14
Sherman-Palladino, Amy: *Marvelous Mrs. Maisel* 75, 109–118
Shining, The 30
sidekick 63
simplicity 14, 16, 116
Sinclair, Upton 79
Singer, Bryan: *The Usual Suspects* 9
Snyder, Blake 69, 78
Soderbergh, Steven 120; *Ocean's Eleven* 69
Sopranos, The 69
"Southern" (as opposed to "Western") film genre 57
spy story 31
stakes 35–45; destiny 43; finite 41; heist film exercise 72, 75, 76–77; *Get Out* 93–94, 95, 97, 98–99; horror film exercise 50, 53, 54, 55, 56; layered 41; *Marvelous Mrs. Maisel* 112, 113, 114, 118; meaningful 40–41; qualities of 40–41; *Portrait* 103, 105, 107–108; property 42–43; social or familial order 42; stories enriched by 36–39; study guide 44–45; superhero exercise 61, 64–65, 66, 67, 58; *Three Will Be Blood* 84–85, 87–88; types of 41–43; well-being of others 42; well-being of own self 41–42
Stanton, Andrew: *Wall-E* 30, 37–38, 84
story: backstory 50, 53, 60, 62, 65, 66, 81, 102; "bad guys" 69; changes experienced by character in 27, 33; consequences in 35; diagramming 44; earning complexity over course of film 16; ending a story 82; failures experienced by characters in 28, 61; GoFaSt model's prioritizing of 10; gritty urban crime 14; *how* and *why* of 81; new story elements 30, 49, 73; origin story, for superhero 67; plot vs. story 21; shorter format screen story 110; superhero 77; theme in 39;

using stakes to modulate scope of 45; *see also* pacing of story
storyline 2; emotional stakes of 42; expanding idea into 12; using GoFaSt model to organize 13
storytelling 4; conventions of, potential for staleness of 68; horror genre of 47; trends in 7; visual 37
storytellers 3
streaming format 6, 7, 24, 109
subplot 7, 9, 40, 89; coming-of-age 49; *Portrait of a Lady on Fire* 106–107
superhero genre 24, 46; GoFaSt exercise 57–68; horror-superhero 47

Tarantino, Quentin: *Django Unchained* 47; *Pulp Fiction* 19, 21, 31, 33, 42
Taxi Driver 43
television writing 7, 109, 111, 116, 121; *see also* Marvelous Mrs. Maisel
There Will Be Blood 16, 22; GoFaSt case study 53, 78–90; notion of stakes in 39; theme of family in 39
three-act structure 3, 5–6, 7, 12, 75, 82, 96, 119–120
thrillers 21, 31, 36, 38; social thriller 91
Treasure of the Sierra Madre, The 19
types of failure *see* failure
types of goals *see* goals
types of stakes *see* stakes

Uncut Gems 41
underdogs 17, 81
Usual Suspects 9

vagueness 15, 82, 104
Vampyr 52
verifiable goal 15–16, 59, 62–4, 96, 105; unverifiable 104
verifiable journey 31
victory, as type of goal 20
Vogler, Christine 119

Wall-E 30, 37–38, 84
weakness, in a character 14, 25, 28, 62, 89
weakness, in a script 2
Weine, Robert: *The Cabinet of Dr. Caligari* 52
well-being of others 42, 44

well-being of own self (as character) 31, 41–42, 115–116
well-being of planet 67, 84
Welles, Orson 73
Wendy and Lucy 28
Western film genre 57
Where is the Friend's House? 17, 84
whodunnits 31, 81
Wilder, Billy 73
Woman Under the Influence 5, 30
Wright, Edgar: *Baby Driver* 69; *Shaun of the Dead* 47

writing a movie (as opposed to another genre) 9–10
writing a new film 47–48
writing outside structural models 4–6
writing process 11–13, 25, 60, 78; rewriting 22
writing within structural models 4

Yan, Cathy: *Birds of Prey* 58

Zemeckis, Robert: *Cast Away* 30

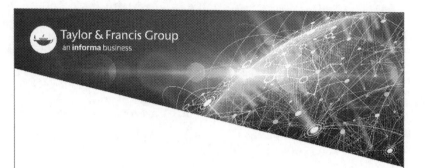

Printed in the United States
by Baker & Taylor Publisher Services